Praise for *Beyond Bath Time*

"At the end of the day, how do you know you've been a good mom? Whose idea of motherhood are you trying to live up to—yours, your friend's, or God's? Can you be a fulfilled follower of Christ in your role as an everyday mama? Our friend Erin has taken on these questions and more in this insightful and captivating read. She has brought to light truths that will impact you and your family for life. Thank you, Erin, for challenging us even in the seemingly mundane, to capture a big vision picture of motherhood. Motherhood matters because it is the heart of God."

— WES and CARRIE WARD, just an everyday dad and mama,
and *Revive Our Hearts'* senior director of media (him!)
and author of *Together: Growing Appetites for God* (her!)

"Authentic. Warm. Inviting. Practical. Insightful. Penetrating. Biblical. *Beyond Bath Time* is all that and more. Erin is a fresh, clear voice with a timely message, developed in the laboratory of life, with God's Word in hand. She challenges women to reclaim motherhood as a high, holy, and purposeful calling—a sacrificial vocation with eternal rewards!"

— NANCY DEMOSS WOLGEMUTH, author,
host of *Revive Our Hearts* radio

"What we often encounter about motherhood seems to be a caricature of real life. Either it's the unattainable super-mom of the advertising industry or the unbelievably inconvenienced cranky mom of sitcoms. Fortunately, Erin Davis gives us a real portrait. But more importantly, she doesn't stay grounded in the daily experience of our lives here. She points us to the eternal purposes of motherhood—purposes that all women share, whether or not we've actually given birth. Read this book to be encouraged, strengthened, and committed to God's wisdom in the beauty of motherhood."

—CAROLYN MCCULLEY, author of *Radical Womanhood: Feminine Faith in a Feminist World* and *Did I Kiss Marriage Goodbye? Trusting God with a Hope Deferred*

"I love how Erin lays out the big picture for moms. She lifts the curtain to see beyond the piles of laundry and provides a peek into the sacred. Erin challenges you to live beyond the daily monotony that threatens to suck the joy from motherhood. *Beyond Bath Time* beautifully portrays motherhood's sacred calling but doesn't sugarcoat the hard places. Erin speaks as a mom who doesn't have all the answers, but is learning how to mother with joy. She hands out good doses of practical help and encouragement while inviting mothers to join her in the high and holy battle."

—KIMBERLY WAGNER, author of *Fierce Women: The Beauty of a Soft Warrior* (September 2012)

"My family does not come before ministy. My family is my first ministry. Erin's book is a reminder to all moms that raising children well and with joy is ministry and the single best way to reach the next generation with God's truth."

—JOSH MCDOWELL, bestselling author and speaker

"In a 'childless by choice' world that measures a woman's worth by her contribution to the paid workforce, motherhood is all too often set aside or given second-class status. But look out . . . here comes Erin Davis! She's on a mission to show you that motherhood matters, and that being a mom might just be the most important thing you'll ever do. If you're a Gen-Xer, who's swallowed the pop culture Kool-Aid, you need to read this book—and consider if the hand that rocks the cradle does, in fact, rule the world!"

—MARY KASSIAN, author of *Girls Gone Wise*

"Revive our hearts" Podcast

Beyond Bath Time
Embracing Motherhood
as a Sacred Role

ERIN DAVIS

MOODY PUBLISHERS
CHICAGO

All Scripture quotations, unless otherwise indicated, are taken from *The Holy Bible, English Standard Version,* Copyright © 2000, 2001 by Crossway Bibles, a division of Good News Publishers. Used by permission. All rights reserved.

Scripture quotations marked NIV 1984, are taken from *The Holy Bible, New International Version*®, NIV®. Copyright © 1973, 1978, 1984 by Biblica, Inc.™ Used by permission of Zondervan. All rights reserved worldwide. www.zondervan.com

Scripture quotations marked NIV, are taken from *The Holy Bible, New International Version*®, NIV®. Copyright ©1973, 1978, 1984, 2011 by Biblica, Inc.™ Used by permission of Zondervan. All rights reserved worldwide. www.zondervan.com

Edited by Jeanette Littleton   Interior Desing: Ragont Design
Cover Design: Rule 29 Creative, Inc.   Author Photo: Sarah Carter Photography
Cover Image: Bubbles: 2ndpic | www.secondpicture.com
        Rubber Duck and Soap: Big Pants Production
        Towels: Irina Fischer
Author Photo: Sarah Carter Photography

Library of Congress Cataloging-in-Publication Data
Davis, Erin
    Beyond bath time: embracing motherhood as a sacred role / Erin Davis
    p. cm.
    ISBN: 978-0-8024-0562-3
    1. Mothers—Religious life. 2. Motherhood— Religious aspects—
Christianity
    BV4529.18.D375 2012

                                            2012005459

All websites and phone numbers listed herein are accurate at the time of publication but may change in the future or cease to exist. The listing of website references and resources does not imply publisher endorsement of the site's entire contents. Groups and organizations are listed for informational purposes, and listing does not imply publisher endorsement of their activities.

We hope you enjoy this book from Moody Publishers. Our goal is to provide high-quality, thought-provoking books and products that connect truth to your real needs and challenges. For more information on other books and products written and produced from a biblical perspective, go to www.moodypublishers .com or write to:

Moody Publishers
820 N. LaSalle Boulevard
Chicago, IL 60610

5 7 9 10 8 6 4

Printed in the United States of America

To my mom—I couldn't write a book about motherhood without shining a white-hot spotlight on the fantastic job my own mom, Gini, has done. Mom, yours are the shoulders on whom all of us rest. When I grow up, I want to be just like you.

Contents

CHAPTER 1:

Welcome to the World, Mom!

Your baby probably won't survive the pregnancy. I suggest you abort him."

These words plunged me deep into the waters of motherhood. I was flailing. I couldn't see the surface. I feared that the swirl of emotions and responsibilities that come with being a mom would swallow me and I had no idea where to look for a life raft.

I was twelve weeks pregnant with my first child. At that point in the pregnancy I hadn't felt much beyond fear, anxiety, and a lot of nausea. My husband and I had planned to start our family, but when the stick turned pink sooner than we expected, I couldn't stop thinking about all the ways my life would change. I broke the news to my husband that a baby was on the way by sitting on our bed in a bathrobe and sobbing.

I didn't have time to be a mom.

Now doctors were telling me my baby wasn't well. Deciding not to abort our tiny son was easy. But I didn't know God would use that decision to teach me His passion for motherhood and to totally remake my heart.

If you are still holding your breath, relax. My son Elisha was born perfectly healthy—miraculously healed from a condition that could have taken him from us. But that healing didn't occur until the day of his birth. For seven long months we waited to find out if our baby would survive.

In that context, motherhood ceases to be about tiny clothes and cuddly blankets. When you don't know if you will even bring your baby home, you spend less time painting the nursery and more time on your knees.

Skipping the warm fuzzies of pregnancy brought me face-to-face with the reality of motherhood. I couldn't imagine how having a child would fit into my routine, my marriage, my hopes for my life, my definition of ministry, and my dreams for the future.

I was simultaneously desperate to hold my baby and terrified of the nuclear bomb that seemed pointed toward my life. When that bomb hit in the form of a healthy baby boy who demanded every second of my time, energy, and emotions, the shock was almost too much for me.

I WAS SIMULTANEOUSLY desperate to hold my baby and terrified of the nuclear bomb that seemed pointed toward my life.

Having It All and Gaining Nothing

My life before baby looked exactly like our culture told me it should. I had multiple degrees from good colleges. I was married to a wonderful man who supported my professional and academic goals. I had a rewarding career as a writer and speaker. My time was my own. My priorities were in line with what I wanted from life. I was a woman of the new millennium.

I had followed the script that had been written for me in a world where women were supposed to "have it all." But it wasn't the fairy tale I'd been promised.

I discovered quickly that academic and vocational success didn't bring lasting fulfillment. I was the center of my universe and my best efforts were directed outside of my home, but most days I felt more exhausted than fulfilled.

This isn't the part in the story where I tell you that I became a Christian and everything changed. I had passionately served Jesus since I was fifteen years old. In fact, my husband and I had initially chosen childlessness because we wanted to serve Christ. We saw children as a burden. We believed that our careers and ministry and marriage were too important to risk the strain children would bring. We didn't feel called to become parents nor did we see parenting as potential ministry.

We had been lied to. It's a lie that has been whispered into many ears.

More and more women are choosing childlessness. Others resent their husbands and children because they see them as burdens, a stumbling block to achieving a higher calling. Motherhood is not revered as a sacred role. Career is king. The modern equation leaves little room for children.

I believe this is one of the greatest tragedies of our time.

It isn't that motherhood is the hidden secret to fulfillment. I didn't hold Elisha for the first time and suddenly decide nothing else mattered. I did discover that my attitude about motherhood pointed to a bigger problem that exists in women's hearts everywhere. We've lost touch with living out our unique design as women. We don't know how to function as we've been created to function.

The Bible shows us that God esteems the roles of wife and mother. Eve's name means "life." The Proverbs 31 woman worked diligently to provide for her household. Jesus opted not to appear on earth as an adult ready to rule. He came through the womb of a mother and was tenderly cared for by His mom throughout His life. God's Word says much about the ministry of motherhood and the value of bearing and nurturing life.

But the issue of motherhood isn't theological. It isn't best explored in the political arena or defined by the talking heads of our culture. The value of motherhood is most important in the heart of every woman.

{ *More WISE Words* }

YEARS AGO, BEFORE this generation of mothers was even born, our society decided where children rank in the list of important things. When abortion was legalized, we wrote it into law. Children rank way below college. Below world travel for sure. Below the ability to go out at night at your leisure. Below honing your body at the gym. Below any job you may have or hope to get. In fact, children rate below your desire to sit around and pick your toes, if that is what you want to do. Below everything. Children are the last thing you should ever spend your time doing. If you grew up in this culture, it is very hard to get a biblical perspective on motherhood, to think like a free Christian woman about your life, your children. How much have we listened to partial truths and half lies? Do we believe that we want children because there is some biological urge, or the phantom "baby itch"? Are we really in this because of cute little clothes and photo opportunities? Is motherhood a rock-bottom job for those who can't do more, or those who are satisfied with drudgery? If so, what were we thinking?

—RACHEL JANKOVIC[1]

Where are you in the journey of motherhood? Are you a new mom struggling to redefine the boundaries of your life among a sea of diapers, feedings, and sleepless nights? Have you been a mom so long that you've lost yourself along the way and you long to know your reach goes beyond car pools and chore charts? Do you understand it's your job to teach your children about spiritual principles but struggle to know how to connect in the chaos? Are you a young woman who's not sure you want children but secretly suspect that the world's not telling the whole truth as it teaches that womanhood is about living like it's all about you?

I'm looking for a few good moms. Moms who will dare to hold on to a view that seems out-of-date and search for God's heart on the issue of motherhood; moms who are willing to see past the endless list of mothering responsibilities to see a bigger, more eternal picture. I'm looking for women who will stand up to the culture and reclaim motherhood as a high and holy calling.

I'm looking for you.

Connecting the Dots

Now it's your turn, my friend! At the end of each chapter we'll have some thought-provoking questions for you to respond to and connect these thoughts to your life. You might consider keeping a journal to jot the answers to these questions and notes on how God is speaking to you about your own journey. Or use these questions as discussion starters as you go through this book with a group of momma friends.

1. How did you feel when you first learned you were going to have a child? Take a few moments to relive the memory.

2. Did those feelings change as you went through the pregnancy?

3. How did your views of motherhood change after you got that little bundle in your arms?

4. What do you feel are your strengths as a mom? Your weaknesses?

CHAPTER 2:

What Makes a Mom?

Motherhood is under attack.

- About half of the public—46 percent in a 2009 Pew Research Center poll—say it makes no difference that a growing number of women don't ever have children.[2]
- Only 9 percent of teenagers say that they definitely plan to become parents in their early adult years.[3]
- Roughly eight in ten women say it's harder to be a mother today than it was thirty years ago.[4]

You may not have realized that a war has been raging over the issue of motherhood, but I bet you've felt battle-weary. Is motherhood for you? Is parenting a worthwhile use of your life? Maybe you're a mom who is caught in the crossfire between your desire for purpose and the bombardment of negative messages about motherhood. Yes, you're a mom and you love your kids, but the endless stream of dirty diapers, discipline hurdles, and battles over bath time leave you feeling unsatisfied in your role. That dissatisfaction is magnified by the culture's message that having a career is the path to lasting fulfillment.

How are we *supposed* to feel about motherhood? And when it comes to defining what makes a mom, whose voices should we listen to?

To answer those questions we have to track how motherhood has been defined through the years. Revisiting history helps us trace the roots of our own struggle to define motherhood.

When we look at the big picture, the problem starts to come into focus. The bottom line is that our culture loves the *idea* of motherhood, but when the baby shower is over, the clear message is that putting your talents, time, energy, and passion toward mothering is a mistake.

OUR CULTURE LOVES the *idea* of motherhood, but when the baby shower is over, the clear message is that putting your talents, time, energy, and passion toward mothering is a mistake.

My friend Cindy put it this way: "Our culture has a split personality. We often put mothers on a pedestal during pregnancy, thinking, 'Oh, how sweet and precious' with visions of lullabies, coos, and baby firsts. But under the surface we feel sorry for the mom-to-be and think of the sleeplessness, dirty diapers, tantrums, and basic upheaval."

How did we get here? When did the idea that motherhood is a high and holy calling start to unravel? Pop in your favorite Beatles CD and let me take you back to the 1960s. Let's look at a little idea called feminism.

You may remember the feminist movement from your American history textbook. It's a campaign that conjures images of women rallying for equality while burning their bras in the name of change. Their mantra became, "Feminism is the radical notion that women are people."

Good stuff, right? As women we want equality, we want opportunities, we want our God-given value to be recognized.

But hidden in the message of feminism is a heap of lies about motherhood. While the headlining message of the movement makes sense, the subtle undertones about marriage, motherhood, and what it means to be a woman don't line up with the truth found in God's Word.

The tidal wave of feminism began when Betty Friedan started asking questions about the role of women. Friedan looked around and concluded that women were unsatisfied. After interviewing these unhappy women, she decided that in order to find happiness, women needed to have a serious career. She promised that meaningful work would fill a vacuum in women's hearts and that they would be fulfilled.

In her bestselling book, *The Feminine Mystique*, Friedan confronted the value of motherhood and dared to ask a question you may have asked yourself.

"The problem lay buried, unspoken, for many years in the

minds of American women. It was a strange stirring, a sense of dissatisfaction, a yearning that women suffered in the middle of the twentieth century in the United States. Each suburban wife struggled with it alone. As she made the beds, shopped for groceries, matched slipcover material, ate peanut butter sandwiches with her children, chauffeured Cub Scouts and Brownies, lay beside her husband at night—she was afraid to ask even herself the silent question—'Is this all?'"[5]

Doesn't part of you want to scream, "Yes!"? Don't the mundane tasks of motherhood seem unfulfilling on the surface? Isn't there a corner in each of our hearts that secretly nags, "Is this all there is?"

Speaking Our Bitterness

The feminist revolution began as a grass-roots movement intentionally constructed to pounce on women's unfulfilled longings. Their methods may surprise you. What eventually became huge rallies of women screaming for equality started in living rooms, under the guise of raising awareness.

This technique can actually be traced to the revolutionary armies of Mao Tse-tung in the earlier part of the twentieth century. Mao's armies would host "speak bitterness meetings" where they allowed women and peasants to vent their frustrations at being downtrodden. The meetings caused bitterness to rise and anger to spread like wildfire. The downtrodden began to revolt. Thanks to the resulting chaos, Mao Tse-tung could take over villages with very little resistance.

The feminist movement used the same strategy. The leaders gathered small groups of women in living rooms and asked questions that provoked and revealed bitterness over the roles of wife and mother. The leaders took something very personal and made it political, promising to create the change that would lead to lasting contentment.

That may feel like a history lesson (don't worry; there won't be a quiz), but I bet you've held your own "speak bitterness" meetings on the subject of motherhood. I'd guess some days you've wondered if motherhood is a barrier to your happiness. Most of us have. But more than fifty years after the feminist revolution, it's clear that we can't find the answer to our dissatisfaction by writing off motherhood.

After all, where has feminism led us?

"Marriages have broken down. Families have broken down. Children are unparented," explains Mary Kassian, author of *The Feminist Mistake*. "And instead of seeing the value of nurturing the next generation and the value of pouring our lives out for others, women now believe unless they are being self-fulfilled and having their lives mean something out there, they will not find fulfillment and happiness."[6]

Motherhood has taken a huge hit, but has the vacuum that Friedan noticed been filled as a result?

"I think, if anything there's more frustration . . . because the dream promised fulfillment and satisfaction for women, but it hasn't delivered," Kassian notes.[7]

Looking Elsewhere for Answers

Relegating motherhood to the bottom of your priority list isn't the answer. And, as it turns out, culture's claim that motherhood is the crux of your longings doesn't hold water. But what can we do with the frustration we feel as we parent? How do we answer Friedan's original question, "Is this all?"

It's a fair question. After all, the tasks of motherhood can certainly seem trivial. How you answer that question in your own heart will determine the trajectory of your mothering journey, but the answer usually doesn't come the first time you hold your baby in your arms.

"IS THIS ALL?" is a fair question. After all, the tasks of motherhood can certainly seem trivial.

Perhaps that's why Paul took the time to address women about the ins and outs of establishing a home. "But as for you, teach what accords with sound doctrine. . . . Older women likewise are to . . . teach what is good, and so train the young women to love their husbands and children, to be self-controlled, pure, working at home, kind, and submissive to their own husbands, that the word of God may not be reviled" (Titus 2:1, 3–5).

What did Paul say about loving our children and working in our homes? These are skills that must be taught! And what curriculum should we use? The solid doctrine found in God's Word.

Did anyone else just breathe a massive sigh of relief?

I don't know about you, but I often find myself flailing because motherhood doesn't happen as naturally as I imagined it would.

When my baby refuses to nurse, when discipline doesn't work, or when my marriage sags under the strain of raising children, I really start to wonder why mothering is worthwhile.

But Paul lets us off the hook. By urging the church to teach women how to mother by using God's Word, he reveals that great mothering is learned and not intuitive. The answer to our longing isn't to ditch mothering or to let our frustration eclipse the satisfaction that can come from raising the next generation. Rather, it comes by doing the hard work of seeking God's truth on mothering, and making the countercultural choice to pursue motherhood as a high and holy calling.

Listen carefully to what I am *not* saying. I am not saying feminists were only slightly off and that motherhood—not career—is the secret to filling the vacuum in our lives. Motherhood for motherhood's sake won't leave us any more fulfilled than working just to work. But understanding your God-given purpose and embracing that purpose does lead to fulfillment. Knowing God's truth and putting it into practice is the only way to fill the void.

This is true no matter what your mothering circumstances look like. Before I go any further, let me speak to those of you who think this book may not be for you because you're not a stay-at-home mom.

I am a working mom who stays at home most of the time with my kids. In that sense I'm a hybrid of a working and stay-at-home mom, but I spend the bulk of my day with my kids. As a result, throughout this book I include many illustrations from that realm. But I know that many of you are working outside the home full-time, and as a result you may be shouldering an extra dose of guilt, stress, and anxiety over the parameters of your role. What a great reason to ask God give you His vision for motherhood. The bottom line is that we all need His truth in this area, regardless of where our clock is punched.

With that in mind, let's ask Friedan's questions again.

Is it just housework, or is it service?

Is it just PB and J, or is it worship?

Is it just a car pool, or is it a mission field?

Is it just raising kids, or is it living out a God-given purpose?

These are important questions—questions the culture will tell you are old-fashioned and reverse progress. They're also questions the Enemy is doing his best to steer you away from.

After all, Betty Friedan wasn't the first to ask, "Is this all?" It's a version of the same question the serpent hissed to the first woman in the garden of Eden. The account reminds us where the battle over motherhood is really being waged:

> The serpent said to the woman, "You will not surely die. For God knows that when you eat of [the tree] your eyes will be opened, and you will be like God, knowing good and evil." So when the woman saw that the tree was good for food, and that it was a delight to the eyes, and that the tree was to be desired to make one wise, she took of its fruit and ate." (Genesis 3:4–6)

The lie was, "You're missing out on something, girl!"

The implication was, "What you have now isn't enough."

The question Satan really dared Eve to ask was, "Is this all?" And Eve started to wonder, "If I nibble on this apple, will I find something more satisfying?"

It's easy to point our finger at the feminists, but the heart of this issue goes back to the beginning. The battle to embrace mother-hood has always been raging and, just like in the garden, the stakes have always been sky-high.

{ *More WISE Words* }

FEMINISM AS A political movement is actually less than two hundred years old, but feminism actually goes all the way back to the dawn of time, right to the garden of Eden, where one woman decided that God's boundaries and definitions for her weren't good and that she could go get what she wanted. And there was a man standing right by her who passively let her do it. The seeds of feminism lie in all of our hearts; they lie in my heart, they lie in everyone's heart, because the seeds of feminism are "I want what I want, I want to define how I want it, and I don't want to give God the glory."

—CAROLYN MCCULLEY.[8]

Pastor and teacher Alistair Begg once said, "The place of a mother is so vital. Get it right and we have great hopes. Get it wrong and we have great fears."[9] This is why the Enemy has set his sights on motherhood. That is why embracing motherhood as a calling is not a battle easily won. Recognizing these stakes should motivate us to pick up the sword of the Spirit, which is God's Word (Ephesians 6:17), and to fight for this vital role.

Maybe you feel as if you've nibbled on a rotten apple yourself. Maybe you've always known that the culture's path to fulfillment is a dead end, but you're still wrestling with how to live motherhood as a God-given calling. Maybe you're still not convinced that motherhood matters but are willing to put the issue through the filter of God's Word.

Wherever you are on the journey to embrace motherhood, I hope you'll join me in the battle. I hope you'll decide that God's plan for motherhood is worth fighting for and that understanding God's plan for you as a mother is worth some work.

Truth's Power to Liberate

Think back to those "speak bitterness meetings" used so powerfully by the feminists and Mao Tse-tung's communist armies and consider this: bitterness isn't the only source of power. Dissatisfaction isn't the only catalyst for change.

What if our liberation isn't found in voicing bitterness and letting it negatively shape our hearts but in seeking God's truth and encouraging one another to be transformed by it? What if by embracing God's plan for who we are as women we find true fulfillment, purpose, and freedom?

I believe it's possible, and it starts with taking Paul's advice from Titus 2 to study motherhood, letting God's Word be our teacher.

Connecting the Dots

1. What specific evidence do you see that the culture has an anti-motherhood mind-set?

2. What impact has this had on your own thoughts about motherhood?

3. In what ways do you speak out bitterness about your role as a mom?

4. Do you feel that family planning is an area that you and your husband have surrendered to Christ? Why or why not?

CHAPTER 3:

Talking Lies over Coffee

Go ahead; pull up a chair. Imagine you're grabbing coffee with a group of my closest friends and me (large caramel latte with extra whip here, please). About the time the caffeine hits, the conversation turns into a no-holds-barred chat about motherhood. We're going to get real about what's going on in our homes and dare to share the secrets of what's brewing in our hearts.

Before we dig too deeply, let me introduce you to the other moms.

At the age of thirty-nine, Cindy left a successful career as a speech pathologist after giving birth to Alistair.

Bekah is the stay-at-home mom of two children under three. She and her husband were childfree for eight years before bringing home their firstborn.

Kristie is the homeschooling mom of four children ages six to fourteen, as well as being a foster mom.

Jordan is a new mom with one bouncing baby girl.

Victoria got pregnant on her honeymoon. Now she's learning to balance motherhood, graduate school, and a job she loves as a high school teacher. I've had a front-row seat to her rapid transformation from single woman to bride to mommy.

These are *great* moms who love the Lord and see the value in raising their children with purpose. But they're breathing the same air as you and me, and sometimes they feel suffocated by the realities of parenting. Some are aware of the lies the culture has told them about motherhood, but struggle to hold on to God's truth; others simply wonder why mothering is so hard.

These women have helped me identify the lies that moms believe. They've done so by seeking God's truth in their own lives and by helping me identify lies wrapped around my heart. I hope their honesty will lead you to discover areas where you've been tricked.

Why does pinpointing lies about motherhood matter? Why should we keep talking about the problem instead of jumping right in to find a solution?

Until we know how we've been deceived, we can't weed out the old lies and replace them with God's truth. We must take this step so our hearts can become fertile soil in which God can plant the seeds of His truth.

So, pour yourself another cup of joe and listen to what other mothers are saying. Use their stories as a mirror to examine your own heart, and be on the lookout for lies that have put roots down in your life.

Lie #1: Motherhood is a roadblock to my happiness.

"I sometimes feel like being a mom hinders my happiness," says Victoria. "My life changed so fast. My husband and I could do anything we wanted before becoming parents. We would go on mini-vacations or spend time with friends. These activities completely changed after our baby's arrival."

Maybe you're not missing vacations or adventurous weekends. But most moms are guilty of thinking that the responsibilities, sacrifices, and demands of motherhood are a giant roadblock on the path to their daily happiness.

Jordan is brutally honest about the fact that she wrestled with this lie in the face of sudden loss. "We'd been married for three years when we started trying to have children. After four to five months, I conceived, and then miscarried at six weeks. We'd only known I was pregnant for a few days when I lost the baby, so the emotional toll was minimal. In fact, I was relieved. And then I felt guilty for being relieved. I knew a baby would completely shake things up and I didn't want things shaken up! I liked my life. We had a cute apartment full of adult things, not baby-proofed. My husband and I had fun going out to eat in the middle of the week and seeing movies back-to-back without worrying about getting home for the baby-sitter. And not to mention the money! While we weren't rich, I liked going out to eat and getting massages. I didn't want to spend that money on diapers and sippy cups."

Jordan eventually got pregnant again and gave birth to a healthy baby girl. But her transition into motherhood wasn't easy. She still wrestled with many of the feelings she admitted to after her miscarriage and, like Victoria, Jordan often felt if she wasn't a mom, she would be so much happier.

This lie can be traced, in part, to the feministic messages that promised equality in the workplace and at home would make all women happy. Clearly, happiness does not hinge on one life choice, whether it is work, marriage, or children. But a deeper root is more likely responsible for sprouting crops of bitterness, disillusionment, and discontentment in many mothers' hearts. Perhaps that's why we see mothers nibbling on this lie all the way back to ancient Jerusalem.

MOST OF US have happiness ADD. We look to education to make us happy, but the fulfillment is short-lived so we look elsewhere. The same thing happens with our marriage, our jobs, and eventually our children. We define happiness as whatever makes us feel good in the moment. When change comes, we blame whatever or whoever keeps us from having what we want when we want it.

In Ezekiel 16:45 and 48, we find God chastising the moms of Jerusalem for their bitterness toward their families: "You are the daughter of your mother, who loathed her husband and her children. . . . As I live, declares the Lord GOD, your sister Sodom and her daughters have not done as you and your daughters have done."

Ouch! God's harsh words put this lie into clear focus. He says the bitterness of these moms toward their husbands and children is worse than the sins of the women of Sodom. You remember them, right? Their sins warranted a punishment of fire and brimstone!

In other words, blaming our husbands and children for our discontentment is a big deal. The hard truth is that most of us have happiness ADD. We look to education to make us happy, but the fulfillment is short-lived so we look elsewhere. The same thing happens with our marriage, our jobs, and eventually our children. We define happiness as whatever makes us feel good in the moment. But when change comes, we blame whatever or whoever keeps us from having what we want when we want it.

The Bible teaches us to pursue a version of bliss that is not impacted by sleepless nights, screaming children, or restricted schedules.

Second Corinthians 12:9–10 says, "But [God] said to me, 'My grace is sufficient for you, for my power is made perfect in weakness.' Therefore I will boast all the more gladly of my weaknesses, so that the power of Christ may rest upon me. For the sake of Christ, then, I am content with weaknesses, insults, hardships, persecutions, and calamities. For when I am weak, then I am strong."

It is easy to blame our children when days don't go exactly as we want, but God's truth shows us we can choose contentment in all circumstances, and that the frustrations of motherhood are actually blessings if they move us to press on in the power of Christ.

Lie #2: Motherhood is defined by the decision whether or not to work.

This is a version of lie #1. We explored what it sounds like when it comes from the mouths of cultural movers and shakers in the previous chapter, but listen to what it sounds like when it comes from real moms.

"When my daughter was first born, I was stuck at home with her," reflects Bekah. "My husband, however, could still do all that he pleased. I felt cheated and left out. Then when I quit my job to stay at home with her, I felt I wasn't using the gifts God had given me as a high school teacher. I felt that I could be doing so much more than sitting at home staring at a sleeping child."

Cindy also grieved the loss of a career.

"I remember when Alistair was around four to five weeks old. The rush of meals, visitors, phone calls, and gifts had slowed. Steve was back to taking long road trips for work, and I felt trapped and isolated. I often stood in the shower crying and praying for peace of mind. Before motherhood, as a speech pathologist I was in the operating room for surgery with an ENT team, mapping out treatments with other specialists, discussing studies with respected radiologists, and evaluating and treating patients. Then, I felt like my identity was gobbled up by this little being who had no sense of schedule."

This is how the negative messages about motherhood rear their ugly heads. These moms didn't buy the whole lie that career was king. After all, they quit their jobs to mother. But when they found motherhood to be demanding, boring, and isolating they were tempted to nibble on the lie that their work outside the home was the real road to fulfillment.

Strangely this lie has a close cousin that lives in contradiction. Many moms who continue working after they have children also wonder if they chose poorly.

So much has been written about working moms versus stay-at-home moms. It's as if deciding when and how to work after baby is the most important question mothers must answer. However, this is not really an issue of staying at home versus working. It's an issue of how we view motherhood at its core.

When moms turn to questions about their potential careers to deal with the frustrations of motherhood, they hop on a hamster wheel that will never reassure them. Moms like Bekah and Cindy wrestle with the lie that their careers will satisfy and think, *If I were working, would I feel this way? Is this a misuse of my gifts? Am I missing out on something better?*

Moms who work often wonder, *If I were home more would life be easier? If I didn't have to work outside the home, would my life feel more balanced?*

These questions keep moms stuck on the pixels instead of seeing the big picture.

Ephesians 2:10 offers important clarity: "For we are his workmanship, created in Christ Jesus for good works, which God prepared beforehand, that we should walk in them."

Because you are God's workmanship, He has prepared good works for you to do. The frustrations of parenting might surprise you, but they don't surprise Him. He knows mothering is tough, and He thinks you can do it anyway.

We have the choice to see our circumstances as an opportunity to do the important work that God has for us or to dwell on the lie that He could use us more efficiently if we were living a different life.

35

The most important question about motherhood isn't, "Should I work outside the home or not?" The most important question is, "Will I allow God to use the circumstances of my life and my family to accomplish great things for His kingdom?" Getting caught up in trying to figure out the perfect balance of work and home distracts many mothers from seeing the plain truth that only God can fill you and use your gifts to achieve maximum gain.

THE MOST IMPORTANT question about motherhood isn't, "Should I work outside the home or not?" It is, "Will I let God use the circumstances of my life and family to accomplish great things for His kingdom?"

Lie #3: The Ultimate Goal of Motherhood Is Perfectionism

Remember Kristie? Homeschooling mom of four and foster parent? She's one of my motherhood idols. She runs her household beautifully and manages to have good hair while doing it. I've never seen her lose her cool. She's a woman who seems to love every part of being a mom.

Kristie mothers well because she sees the value in making her family her top priority. Yet she admits that she's felt the sting of our culture's obsession with perfectionism, especially when it comes to motherhood.

"I hear two main messages from our culture: first, that motherhood is a distraction, an interruption from what should be important to me—mainly myself and a career. Second, if a woman does choose motherhood, the only way for it to have meaning or value is to do it better than anyone else, to be a supermom who perfectly balances career, cooking, chauffeuring, cleaning, personal time, and date nights . . . a supermom who has a perfect house, perfect husband, perfect job, and perfect kids—because if you're going to focus on motherhood, it is only worthwhile if everything is perfect."

You feel the pressure to mother perfectly, too, don't you? We all do. And the lie that perfection is the goal of mothering—or is even possible—has put many of us in bondage.

Where did the lie that perfection is the key to unlocking meaningful mothering come from? In part, we can blame celebrities who flaunt their post-baby bodies by wearing bikinis on the cover of *People* magazine or coo over how easily they've adjusted to life as a mom while handing their baby to an entourage of aides offscreen. Star moms have PR firms, agents, and hair and makeup staffers who help them generate an unrealistic image of motherhood. We know the image they are selling us is bogus, yet we feel we should strive for it.

But Hollywood is not the ultimate propagator of this lie. A part of each of us wants to forget who we are at our core—specifically that we are prone to sin and desperately need God's grace and help in our hearts and lives.

James 3:2 says, "For we all stumble in many ways."

Paul knew this truth well. He wasn't a mother, but he understood what it was like to be in a tug-of-war between his desire for perfection and his inability to achieve it. In Romans 7:19–20, he said, "I do not do the good I want, but the evil I do not want is what I keep on doing. Now if I do what I do not want, it is no longer I who do it, but sin that dwells within me."

Maybe Paul understood motherhood after all.

I want to be a perfect mom who achieves perfect balance and raises perfect kids, but I cannot do it, no matter how hard I try. That's because I am not perfect and never can be. But we can find great hope when we confront this lie with God's truth.

In Philippians 3:12, we read of Paul coming to terms with his imperfections. "Not that I have already obtained this or am already perfect, but I press on to make it my own, because Christ Jesus has made me his own."

You cannot mother perfectly. But that should never have been the goal. You can mother with purpose because Christ has promised that where you are weak He is strong.

In fact, I want to encourage you to make 2 Corinthians 12:9 your new motherhood mantra: "But he said to me, 'My grace is sufficient for you, for my power is made perfect in weakness.' Therefore I will boast all the more gladly of my weaknesses, so that the power of Christ may rest upon me."

How would your world change if you let yourself move away from the notion that you need to mother perfectly and toward the radical idea that motherhood challenges are a gift because they clear a path for God to work in and through you?

Lie #4: If You Can't Stand the Heat, Remodel the Kitchen.

You won't find any quotes from my friends in this section. That's because this lie has consequences so devastating that no one wants to talk about it. There's a sense in our culture that because motherhood is so tough, we're entitled to do whatever it takes to cope. For instance:

- A survey revealed that nearly half of American mothers are unhappy and one-fourth of women are clinically depressed.[10]
- The number of "cocktail moms" who regularly drink to help themselves cope with the demands of motherhood are on the rise.[11]
- Forty-two percent of moms would rather have more money than spend time with their kids.[12]

It would be nice to think these numbers don't reflect the hearts and lives of Christian moms, but that simply isn't the case. Many moms I know are medicated for depression and anxiety. Others turn to food to cope. Some spend money they don't have on items they don't need. And others stay busy so they don't have to face their fears and doubts about motherhood.

Ultimately, this lie has led some mothers to feel justified in walking away from motherhood. These women make choosing to leave their children sound like a liberating and logical choice, as if they're bold enough to chase their dreams.

Surely the soccer moms you know wouldn't dream of leaving their children, right?

I met recently with women's ministry leaders from around the country, and one pastor's wife asked us to pray for moms in her church who are so fed up with the demands they face that some have left their husbands and children for greener pastures.

While it's not common, real moms *are* walking away from their children. Instead of pushing back, more often than not the culture seems to offer these women a book deal.

You may not be dreaming of leaving your family, but do you check out in other ways? Do you spend hours online or disengaged or angry in your attempt to cope with motherhood? If so, you're not alone. Many women seek to deal with motherhood in ways that aren't helpful, healthy, or eternity minded.

What's the bottom line? Young Christian moms have no biblical framework to understand the role that consumes much of their days. As a result, we are flailing.

Moms who turn to substances or shopping or leave their families have vast and varied reasons. But it is worth noting that this is a dark area of deception.

God never gives us a permission slip to do whatever it takes to feel good. In fact, 1 Thessalonians 5:15–24 gives us the opposite instructions:

> See that no one repays anyone evil for evil, but always seek to do good to one another and to everyone. Rejoice always, pray without ceasing, give thanks in all circumstances; for this is the will of God in Christ Jesus for you. Do not quench the Spirit. Do not despise prophecies, but test everything; hold fast what is good. Abstain from every form of evil.
>
> Now may the God of peace himself sanctify you com-

pletely, and may your whole spirit and soul and body be kept blameless at the coming of our Lord Jesus Christ. He who calls you is faithful; he will surely do it.

The culture may teach that we are entitled to do whatever we want to help us deal with our role, but God's Word says to do what is right, to rejoice always, to pray continually, to give thanks regardless, to hold on to what is good, to run away from evil, to grab the promise that God is faithful and hold on for dear life.

Lie #5: Motherhood Will Make You Holy

It seems counterintuitive that this lie would be on the list with the other four. But if we simply focus on the motherhood lies told by our culture, we risk swinging the pendulum in the opposite direction. The truth is that being a mom won't make you more holy, and simply bearing children won't give your life purpose. You don't become a better person with each baby you bring home.

The notion that being a mom makes you holy reminds me of a zinger Jesus threw at the Pharisees in Matthew 23:27. "Woe to you, scribes and Pharisees, hypocrites! For you are like whitewashed tombs, which outwardly appear beautiful, but within are full of dead people's bones and all uncleanness."

The Pharisees were so wrapped up in doing things that made them look good to others that they didn't deal with their stinky hearts. They tried to earn the status of "holy" by following rules, and that didn't work.

In the same way, being a mom, even a great mom, won't earn you preferred parking in heaven or automatically deepen your relationship with Christ.

Only God can make you holy.

Galatians 2:20–23 says, "I have been crucified with Christ. It is no longer I who live, but Christ who lives in me. And the life I now live in the flesh I live by faith in the Son of God, who loved me and gave himself for me. I do not nullify the grace of God, for if righteousness were through the law, then Christ died for no purpose."

Christ's death was sufficient to reconcile you to Him. You don't have to earn His grace, and you don't have to prove you're a serious Christian by trying to win the mother-of-the-century award.

Likewise, no one owes you anything because you've chosen to mother. It's important to realize that a sense of entitlement—feeling that God, your husband, your children, or the world owes you something because you are mothering and it's tough—can mess with your head and heart.

In contrast, committing your mothering to the Lord and seeking His purposes as you mother creates a panoramic view of what you're doing that can move you beyond your sacrifices and help you cope.

It may feel like a subtle nuance, but mothering because you want to pass along the hope you've found in Christ instead of doing so to earn more grace or favor can radically change how you feel about and respond to your role as mother.

{ *More WISE Words* }

TRUTH IS NOT merely an idea or philosophy. Truth is a person—the Lord Jesus Christ. He said of Himself, "I am the way, and the truth, and the life" (John 14:6). True freedom is found in a vital, growing relationship with the Lord Jesus. He has revealed himself (the living Word of God) in the Scriptures (the written Word of God). Staying close to both the living and the written Word of God, will bring you freedom!

—NANCY LEIGH DEMOSS and DANNAH GRESH.[13]

Clearly, when it comes to motherhood, plenty of land mines exist that we risk stepping on. It's easy to be deceived, and the results of believing lies can be disastrous. So, what can you do about it?

First, you can recognize the lies you've believed as a mom. Ask God and wise mothers to help you with this step.

Then, do the hard work necessary to focus on God's vision for motherhood. No simple solutions exist. We can't wave a magic wand and change the culture or reprogram ourselves away from lies and toward God's truth.

But this is where this book gets good. For the next several chapters we will focus on the solution by digging deeply into what God's Word teaches about motherhood.

So let's keep the coffee flowing and the honest conversation rolling. With hearts made freshly fertile by the uprooting of lies, we are ready for God to plant the seeds of His truth.

"So Jesus said to the Jews who had believed him, 'If you abide in my word, you are truly my disciples, and you will know the truth, and the truth will set you free'" (John 8:31–32).

Connecting the Dots

1. What is your biggest secret about being a mother? Don't worry; I won't tell!

2. What lies about mothering do you most identify with from this chapter?

3. What are your gifts as a person—those things you'd highlight if you were going for a new job? What are some ways those gifts do or could enhance your mothering?

4. Have you ever felt the need to be a perfect mom? In what ways? What's one area in your mothering where you can relax your own expectations this week?

5. What do you feel is God's purpose for you in mothering?

CHAPTER 4:

Choosing Childlessness

It's not your imagination—you've been invited to fewer baby showers lately. That's because couples are delaying the decision to have children and are choosing to remain childless. You may be shaving your budget for pink and blue tissue paper, but have you sifted your own choices about if, when, and how many children to have through the filter of God's Word? Is it possible that the constant drip of messages about motherhood has tainted your worldview and your family plan more than you realize?

Maybe you or someone you know has a story that sounds something like this:

My friend Amber loves the Lord and is crazy about her new hubby. When pressed about starting a family, Amber says she wants the freedom to spend as much time with her husband as possible however they desire, such as late-night runs for their favorite scoop of ice cream.

Another friend, Jacqueline, doesn't want children because she wants a ministry. In her mind, that looks like using her time, efforts, talents, and energy to help others outside her home.

Laura is smart and talented and gifted with abilities to organize, cast vision, and lead. She loves her job and feels having kids or staying home to raise them seems like a waste of her talents and passions.

Or maybe your story sounds like mine. My husband and I chose childlessness for seven years because we wanted the freedom to build our lives around reaching teenagers for Christ. That meant spending most evenings at sporting events, taking teens on weekend trips and retreats, and having an open-door policy that wouldn't work well if we had little ones toddling around.

Tipping the Apple Cart

Our culture puts a premium on the right of individuals and couples to choose their lifestyles. The idea that God's Word takes a stand on childbearing that hinders total freedom of choice won't be met with a standing ovation. Because our flesh tends to fight for our own "rights," even those of us who trust the Bible may bristle at the premise that having children is not a choice we should base strictly on our own desires.

Since we've already tipped the apple cart, let's dare to ask the big questions. Does God's mandate to Adam and Eve in the garden to "be fruitful and multiply" (Genesis 1:28) apply to us today? Is living child-free a choice outside of the realm of God's will? And if so, is this a horn Christian moms need to sound?

If you're already a mom, it might feel like a moot point. But it's worth taking the time to talk about the issue of childlessness, because we moms need to be able to engage with other women who are child-free by choice or because of their circumstances.

And let's be honest. Just because we're moms doesn't mean we grasp why the choice to parent matters. Even after we're well into the throes of motherhood, it's worth our time to learn how to defend our position on motherhood in kingdom terms.

EVEN AFTER WE'RE well into the throes of motherhood, it's worth our time to learn how to defend our position on motherhood in kingdom terms.

At this point I'd like to ask you to dig out some closed-toed shoes that will protect you from bruising in case I step on some toes. At the very least, please stop and pray for God to open your heart and mind to *His* truth as you read this chapter. Ask Him to help you to discern between the lies of culture, the cravings of your human nature, and His will for your family.

Just the Facts

Among all women ages forty to forty-four, about 18 percent (or 1.9 million) were childless in 2008. That's up from 10 percent, or nearly 580,000, in 1976.[14]

The choice to live child-free is gaining popularity. According to the US Census Bureau, childlessness among women of childbearing age has increased by nearly 5 percent in the past decade.[15]

Many celebrities have been open about their jump on the childless bandwagon, and make it sound as trendy as a designer handbag.

"I could not . . . have had this life and lived it with the level of intensity that is required to do this show the way it's done," Oprah Winfrey once said about her choice not to have children. "I'd be one of those people that the kid's coming and saying, 'Mom, you've neglected me.' . . . So I have no regrets . . . about not having children."

Actress Cameron Diaz once said, "I think women are afraid to say that they don't want children because they are going to get shunned. But I think that's changing too now. I have more girlfriends who don't have kids than those who do. And honestly? We don't need any more kids. We have plenty of people on this planet."[16]

Childlessness and the Church

So fewer women are having children, not because they *can't* have babies, but because they choose not to. What, if anything, should we say to these women?

If you think that sounds like an issue the church shouldn't touch with a ten-foot pole, you're not alone. We tend to think baby business is so personal we should never discuss it outside our homes.

Conceiving, bearing, and birthing children *is* intimate stuff. In the church we tend to put a premium on modesty and discretion—and rightfully so—where pop culture tends to thrive on talking about anything and everything.

Perhaps that's why those who reject God's heart for motherhood seem to say more about this subject than those of us in the church. The culture says plenty about a woman's right to choose. The media sends a clear message that children are a burden, and if you don't feel like shouldering that burden, you don't have to. Child-free celebrities make childlessness sound noble and glamorous.

THE MEDIA SENDS a clear message that children are a burden, and if you don't feel like shouldering that burden, you don't have to.

As a result, we moms end up second-guessing whether or not we've made the right choice and avoid talking to non-moms about the value of mothering.

Author Rachel Jankovic described the struggle this way:

Years ago, before this generation of mothers was even born, our society decided where children rank in the list of important things. When abortion was legalized, we wrote it into law.

Children rank way below college. Below world travel for sure. Below the ability to go out at night at your leisure. Below honing your body at the gym. Below any job you may have or hope to get. In fact, children rate below your desire to sit around and pick your toes, if that is what you want to do. Below everything. Children are the last thing you should ever spend your time doing.

If you grew up in this culture, it is very hard to get a biblical perspective on motherhood, to think like a free Christian woman about your life, your children.[17]

Because we don't know how to talk about why motherhood matters, it's hard for any of us to know where we stand. And if we choose to have babies because we want to decorate a nursery, fit in with mommy friends, or check off the next "to do" on the list the world has written for us, we will find ourselves in a tailspin.

Likewise, if we encourage our non-mom friends to have children for reasons that aren't eternal, we make a huge mistake. The only solution is to look at God's truth and to let that truth shape "the thoughts and intentions of [our] heart[s]" (Hebrews 4:12).

So, let's roll up our sleeves and start digging into the heart of the matter.

What's My Motivation?

Laura S. Scott, author of *Two is Enough: A Couple's Guide to Living Childless by Choice*, described her motivation to remain childless this way:

My decision to remain childless was motivated in part by fear— fear of regret. I was afraid to take the risk that I might be a bitter, unhappy, or regretful mom . . . particularly when I started hearing from parents who felt compelled to speak out, saying things like "You're lucky not to have kids. They will break your heart." . . . I came away from those hushed confessions feeling like I was privy to the best-kept secret in the world: A surprising number of outwardly happy parents have misgivings or regrets about parenthood.[18]

Laura's not alone. A quick Google search shows dozens of blogs devoted to celebrating "childfreedom" and the "child-free life." These outlets promote childlessness as a lifestyle choice made by proud women of the new millennium. One such blog listed the top one hundred reasons to remain child-free. Here's a sample of the reasoning:

- "You will be happier and less likely to suffer from depression."
- "You will have the capacity and time for meaningful, engaging, quality adult relationships."
- "You will be able to save for a comfortable retirement."
- "You can fully pursue and develop your career."
- "You can fully pursue your educational goals."
- "Your identity will remain firmly intact."
- "You will get a full night's sleep every night."
- "You will stay engaged and informed in current events and will remain an interesting conversationalist."[19]

Do you hear a theme, a drumbeat that echoes throughout this list? Listen closely. "Me. Me. Me." It's a drumbeat that we all must fight against.

I still long for many things on this list. I'd love to use my income on chunky jewelry instead of diapers. I'd be thrilled to have meaningful, adult conversations uninterrupted by toddler tantrums, and at times I'd offer a limb for a night of uninterrupted sleep.

But is building a life based solely on what I want really all it's cracked up to be?

If we look to the Bible, we find that making choices rooted in selfishness, fear, or comfort is not the life God calls us to. There's no doubt that motherhood requires sacrifice. But as Christians, can we justify running away from parenting because of that?

In Romans 12:1–3, we find an interesting progression of verses speaking to the way Christ's followers should approach life.

Romans 12:1 says, "I appeal to you therefore, brothers, by the mercies of God, to present your bodies as a living sacrifice, holy and acceptable to God, which is your spiritual worship."

How does God want you to worship Him? By fighting the self-serving nature of your flesh and choosing to live sacrificially.

Is pregnancy a sacrifice? Yes. Are sleepless nights, restricted schedules, and child-friendly financial choices a strain? You betcha. But is it possible that sacrificing yourself in this way honors God and shapes you into someone more like Him?

Romans 12:2 offers another angle. "Do not be conformed to this world, but be transformed by the renewal of your mind, that by testing you may discern what is the will of God, what is good and acceptable and perfect."

Read that passage again. Let it marinate.

Is the decision to remain child-free actually a choice to conform to the world's insistence that you are the most important factor to consider when making choices? I'm not suggesting we point at non-moms and call them selfish. Instead, we need to acknowledge that living as though God is the center of the universe and we are not produces rewards that outlast a fat retirement account. This reminder benefits moms and non-moms alike.

The truth that it's not about us can be a difficult pill to swallow. "Christian mothers carry their children in hostile territory," says Jankovic. "When you are in public with them, you are standing with, and defending, the objects of cultural dislike. You are publicly testifying that you value what God values, and that you refuse to value what the world values. . . ."[20]

When it comes to parenting, many of us need our minds renewed by God's truth. When we refuse to conform to the world's patterns and lay down our own desires so we can be transformed by the truth, we can discern God's perfect will for our hearts and homes.

Romans 12:3 puts the nail in the coffin of the argument for choosing to live child-free simply out of a desire to live as we want. "For by the grace given to me I say to everyone among you not to think of himself more highly than he ought to think, but to think with sober judgment, each according to the measure of faith that God has assigned."

Don't think of yourself more highly than you should. You are not the only person to consider. Your career, your bank account, your free time, your fears, your worries, and your relationships shouldn't be the only factors in your decisions about motherhood.

The real question isn't, "Is choosing childlessness biblical?" but "Is living for myself biblical? Is ascribing to the world's priorities biblical? Is the choice to remain child-free rooted in the flesh?"

Layers of questions related to this topic are worth asking. For example, are there good reasons to prevent childbearing through the use of birth control? If so, when? Do God's words to Eve in the garden mean every married woman must have children? How many? What about for ministry purposes? Is it wise to forgo biological children to fulfill a specific calling God has on your life?

THE REAL QUESTION isn't, "Is choosing childlessness biblical?" but, "Is living for myself biblical? Is ascribing to the world's priorities biblical? Is the choice to remain child-free rooted in the flesh?"

While I do think God values parenting and calls us to mother, I can't tell you when you should have children, how many, and if you're justified in forgoing motherhood, even for a season. I'm not saying, "All fertile women must have oodles of children immediately!"

But I am saying that in this area, many of us seem to check our faith at the door. In fact, you may have made the same colossal mistake my husband and I made. We prayed extensively about whether or not to get married. We've prayed about what jobs to take and which house to buy. But we *never* prayed about God's will for the size of our family.

By forgoing prayer and Bible study and neglecting to seek wise, Christian guidance in this area of our lives, we were essentially saying that the decision to have children was ours to control. Not until after I became a mom did I realize I had never surrendered this area of my life to the Lord. When it came to the issue of family planning, I simply didn't trust God's sovereignty to provide for my good.

Many of us have made the same mistake Eve made in the garden. We are willing to accept others' viewpoints—in her case, the serpent—without checking with God. We want motherhood on our terms and aren't interested in seeking God's plan if it doesn't match our own.

Though I can't answer your tough questions, I can remind you that our culture values the freedom and opportunities of the "childfree" life. So to reject what the world values and to embrace biblical motherhood—to pour yourself out for another—is truly kingdom work.

Most of you picked up this book because you *aren't* childless. You're a mom, but perhaps you've never thought through God's purposes for child rearing, and motherhood is sucking you dry.

If that's the boat you're in, you may still be a victim of the lie that life is all about you. This lie tends to plant a bitter root in our hearts that sprouts and starts to grow just about the time the contractions begin.

There are also plenty of wrong reasons to have children and, frankly, many of them are equally rooted in selfishness. Let's call selfishness what it is—a plain old nasty sin that we need to deal with. Having children to fill your need for human connection, as a measure of status, as a means to affirm your own worth, or one of the other selfish reasons will inevitably bite back. This isn't a linear equation. You won't decide to have children for all the right reasons once and then be set for the duration of your mothering journey.

So when it comes to motherhood, why is it so difficult to keep our hearts pure? Perhaps it's because the world tries to sell us a bill of goods in this area. Here's an even bolder question: Is it possible that Satan has a stake in whether or not you choose to have kids?

In *Lies Women Believe*, author Nancy Leigh DeMoss helps us understand why the Enemy is bent on convincing us that living child-free is the path to total freedom or that children are stones hanging around our necks.

> God is the Creator, Author, and Giver of life. Not surprisingly, as the sworn enemy of God, Satan hates life. He has always sought to destroy it. He persuaded Adam and Eve to eat of the forbidden fruit, knowing that if they did, they would die, as God had promised. When Adam and Eve gave birth to two sons, Satan incited the elder of the two to murder his younger brother. Satan is the thief Jesus spoke of who "comes only to steal and *kill and destroy*" (John 10:10, italics added). His intent and strategy are precisely the opposite of God's plan, for in the same verse Jesus says, "I have come that they may have *life*, and have it to the full." As a destroyer of life, Satan is definitely not into encouraging childbearing. Every child that is born has the potential to thwart his purposes by receiving God's grace and becoming a subject of the kingdom of God. So anything that hinders or discourages women from fulfilling their God-given calling to be bearers and nurturers of life furthers Satan's efforts.[21]

I hope your toes are starting to uncurl, but your fists are beginning to ball up. There is reason to be angry. As women, we've been lied to for a very long time. An Enemy seeks to use our wombs, our hearts, and our homes to dampen the message of life that Christ came to bring.

Thinking Long Term

In Genesis 1:28, God told Adam and Eve to "be fruitful and multiply and fill the earth and subdue it." In other words, "Find some fig leaves and start sewing some onesies. I intend for you to have babies. Lots of them."

But that mandate was just for Adam and Eve, right? If they had chosen childlessness, the human race would have been a sprint. The future of all humanity doesn't rest on your shoulders. Your decisions about mothering don't really matter to anyone but you, right?

What if we all felt this way? Specifically, what if more and more Christians continue to feel as though giving and nurturing life is someone else's job?

Let's think globally for a minute:

- Worldwide, there are six million fewer children under age six than there were in 1990.[22]
- Some religious groups are dramatically out-breeding others.
  - Mormonism is growing by 40 percent every decade, mainly due to large families.[23]
  - The Population Reference Bureau stated, "The number of Muslims worldwide is projected to grow over the next decade to reach one-quarter of the world's population, largely because of higher fertility among Muslim populations."[24]

— The American Amish have grown from a few thousand a century ago to more than 300,000 now, even though few people join them from the outside.[25]

Economist Robert J. Samuelson wrote, "It's hard to be a great power if your population is shriveling."[26]

He was talking about the nations of Europe, but let's translate his logic to a different kind of kingdom.

In Matthew 28:19–20, Jesus said, "Go therefore and make disciples of all nations, baptizing them in the name of the Father and of the Son and of the Holy Spirit, teaching them to observe all that I have commanded you. And behold, I am with you always, to the end of the age."

Have you ever thought of parenting as discipleship? Or as a way to fulfill the Great Commission?

Imagine if every Christian couple determined to "be fruitful and multiply" by having children and then made discipling those children a top priority.

Imagine if looking through the filter of God's Word helped you to see mothering as kingdom work instead of as a roadblock.

These are possibilities the world says are silly and that the Enemy seeks to steer you away from. But when women choose childlessness or have children without grasping why it matters, the stakes are sky-high.

{ *More WISE Words* }

AS MOTHERS, WOMEN have the opportunity to influence the next generation by spending hours a day for multiple years in the span of their children's lifetime pouring in truth, inspiring hearts and minds to live for God's glory, and training them as change-agents for the next generation—kind of like raising little "radicals for Jesus!"

—KIM WAGNER[27]

Choosing to intentionally disciple the next generation is a high and holy calling for *all* women. Laying down yourself for others and walking into the fire so that God can refine you will separate you from those who don't know Jesus. It will also ultimately draw them to Him.

It's a choice that's countercultural. It flies in the face of everything the world tells us to hold on to and pursue. But make no mistake—it's not about nurseries, tiny clothes, or your personal timetable. It's about the gospel. That reality makes children a choice worth making.

Connecting the Dots

1. Why do you think God set us up in families?

2. Do you know anyone who thinks that parenting is nothing but a big roadblock to "real life"? If you could say anything to such a person, what would you say?

3. What sacrifices have you made to be a momma? Have you ever resented the changes in your life? Explain.

4. How can raising children be an act of worship to God?

CHAPTER 5:

The Lesson Eve Teaches about Legacy

When it's time to hand out mother-of-the-year awards, few of us would think to nominate Eve.

You know: Eve. Wife of Adam. Mom of Cain, Abel, and Seth. And unfortunately for all of us, the one who disobeyed God and was the first person tricked into sinning with one bite of forbidden fruit.

Eve's entire story is told in only four chapters of Genesis. She was created, she sinned, she was banished, she bore children, her children sinned, and then she died.

It may not sound like the makings of a Hallmark Mother's Day special, but Eve's story is not as simple or as tragic as it seems. She can teach us much about who we are. So let's look at where God's vision for parenting was first birthed and see what we can learn about motherhood from the first woman to ever live.

The Mother of Us All

Then the Lord God said, "It is not good that the man should be alone; I will make him a helper fit for him." Now out of the ground the Lord God had formed every beast of the field and every bird of the heavens. . . . But for Adam there was not found a helper fit for him.

So the Lord God caused a deep sleep to fall upon the man, and while he slept took one of his ribs and closed up its place with flesh. And the rib that the Lord God had taken from the man he made into a woman and brought her to the man. Then the man said,

> "This at last is bone of my bones
> and flesh of my flesh;
> she shall be called Woman
> because she was taken out of Man."
> —Genesis 2:18–23

Despite all that was available to him, Adam was lonely. God created Eve to meet Adam's unique needs for companionship, friendship, and family. And although Adam's first attempt to name his bride won't win any awards for originality (v. 23), his second name for her is our first taste of the beauty of motherhood (Genesis 3:20).

Eve's name sounds like the Hebrew word for *life-giver* and resembles the word for *living*. That's fitting since she is the mother of us all.

In his classic The Chronicles of Narnia series, C. S. Lewis reminds us of this truth when he refers to Susan and Lucy Pevensie as the "daughters of Eve." We may want to distance ourselves from Eve, much like a tween on her first day of middle school ("No kisses, Mom, puh-lease!"). Just like most of us realized how cool our own moms are about the time we delivered our own bundles into the world, if we look closely, we find Eve can teach us much about the beauty and power of being moms.

When was Eve first given her name of "life-giver"? Let's do a quick recap. In Genesis 3, Eve was deceived (vv. 1–5). Eve sinned (v. 6). Adam and Eve hid from God and were confronted by Him (vv. 7–13). Then Adam and Eve were cursed (vv. 16–19). Now pay close attention to Adam's very first words after God's punishment was handed down. "The man called his wife's name Eve, because she was the mother of all living" (Genesis 3:20).

Huh? She just blew it big time, and Adam's response was to give Eve a new name that highlighted her ability to give birth?

In Genesis 5:4, we learned that Eve became the mother to many sons and daughters. The Bible does not tell us how many children were born to Adam and Eve, but considering Adam's 930-year life span (Genesis 5:5), we can assume there were many. Think about the fact that there was no birth control, then divide 930 years by nine months. Whew!

Prone to discontentment, unsure of her role, and easily manipulated, Eve was typical of us all. The curse shines a spotlight on the predicament most of us face as we mother.

In Genesis 3:16, God said, "I will surely multiply your pain in childbearing; in pain you shall bring forth children."

The pain of mothering was part of Eve's punishment for sin. From the moment she left the garden, having children would include sorrow for all daughters of Eve.

In light of the curse, Eve could have defaulted to her tendency to wrestle with discontentment, but she didn't. In Genesis 4:1, we read Eve's words after giving birth to her first son, Cain: "With the help of the Lord, I have brought forth a man" (NIV).

You can almost hear the wonder in her voice. But Eve's troubles didn't end with Cain's birth. As a result of her firstborn's sin, Eve became the first mom to bury her child (Genesis 4:8). Furthermore, she mothered without advice from her own mom, other moms, or any of the *What to Expect* books. But we never find her wallowing.

In Genesis 4:25 she became the mother to Seth, and she said, "God has granted me another child, in place of Abel, since Cain killed him" (NIV).

In both recorded birthing accounts, we hear gratitude as she gives credit where credit is due.

"With the help of the Lord . . ." (4:1 NIV).

"God has granted me another child . . . " (4:25 NIV).

We know Eve could be insecure, discontent, and swayed by others. We often prove we are her descendents by repeating those mistakes. But Eve recognized God's hand in her role as a mother. And she shows us our choice: we can focus on our pain or loss or frustration, or we can praise God for the unique joy of bringing forth new life.

Eve knew the sorrow of childbirth. Every contraction reminded her of how badly she missed the mark. Every pang reminded her of how much she lost in the garden. But each little baby face was a testament that she did not lose God, and she did not lose her roles as wife and mother.

Why did Adam remind Eve that she was the mother of all the living on the heels of the curse? Because her sin was not the sum of her legacy.

Let's go back to the birthing room where Seth was born. "God has appointed for me another offspring instead of Abel, for Cain killed him" (Genesis 4:25).

What was the result?

"To Seth also a son was born, and he called his name Enosh. *At that time people began to call upon the name of the Lord*" (4:26, emphasis mine).

Yes, Adam and Eve's sin was passed down to every generation. But that's not all they've given us. The part of Eve's story that we tend to overlook is that her children and grandchildren called on the name of the Lord. These first humans had no outreach events, youth pastors, or vacation Bible schools. Adam and Eve were responsible to build their family on the foundation of knowing and serving the God who created them. Eve told her children about God, and they told their children, and they told their children.

THE PART OF Eve's story that we tend to overlook is that her children and grandchildren called on the name of the Lord.

Yes, generations of sin can be traced back to her, but so can generations of moms who give God glory for the gift of mothering and use motherhood as a platform to tell of the good things He has done.

I don't want to minimize Eve's sin. Sin is serious. It permeates the way we relate to our children and how they relate to us. But Eve's decision to sin in the garden of Eden is just one tune we should sing about the mother of us all. If we look at the big picture, her children were her opus.

Roll Call of Mothers

Eve is not the only mother who speaks to us about the power of legacy. Throughout the Bible we find stories of women who, like Eve, were not perfect but still made a difference in God's kingdom, primarily through their role as mothers. Here are a few of my favorites.

Sarah

Sarah became a mother in her nineties. Her son, Isaac, fulfilled God's promise to build nations through Sarah and her husband, Abraham. But Sarah was impatient with God's promises. She tried to make motherhood work according to her own agenda. There's a lesson for us all in the outcome. But her impatience was not her legacy.

Bathsheba

Bathsheba became a mom under difficult circumstances. After King David saw her and called her to his bedroom, she learned she was carrying a child that did not belong to her husband. David had Bathsheba's husband killed, and as a result of David's sin, the child died. These mothering circumstances would make any of us feel defeated. But Bathsheba later gave birth to Solomon, who became the wisest man in Israel. We can assume Solomon's mother had something to do with his knowledge about God. Mothering was hard for Bathsheba and came at a heavy price, but her loss was not her legacy.

Hannah

Hannah could not get pregnant and desperately wanted a baby. She went to the temple and wailed to the Lord so intensely that the priest thought she was drunk. Hannah promised God that if He gave her a son, she would dedicate that son to His service, to live in the temple.

When Hannah's baby boy arrived, she made a mothering decision more difficult than any I've ever made—she kept her promise. The Bible tells us she raised her miraculous firstborn only until he was weaned, and then she took him to live with Samuel, the priest. We know Hannah still tenderly mothered the baby she could not keep because the Bible tells us that every year Hannah took her boy a "tiny coat." She didn't even get to live with the son for whom she had pined and prayed. She clearly didn't mother for a personal pay-off.

Hannah first ached for a son and then had to deal with living without him. But, Hannah's unmet desires were not her legacy.

{ *More WISE Words* }

WHEN I STAND to give an account before the Lord Jesus Christ and have the opportunity to lay my crowns at His feet, the most valuable

crowns I will have to offer will not be the
conferences where I have spoken or the books I
have written. The most precious gifts that I am
working on for the Lord Jesus every single day of
my life are my children. . . . They have been the
reservoir into which I have invested my energies
and creativity—my life.

—Dorothy Kellel Patterson [28]

The Canaanite Woman

On only a few occasions does Jesus declare that someone has "great faith." One of those times concerned a mom known only as the "Canaanite Woman" (Matthew 15:21–28; Mark 7:24–30). Her daughter was oppressed by a demon and she annoyed the disciples with requests for help. Eventually she got to Jesus and begged Him to heal her daughter.

The Bible tells us that because the Canaanite woman fought for her daughter by running to Jesus, her young girl was healed instantly. Her faith was shown through her mothering, and Jesus responded to her request. Her legacy was not a sick child, but a faith that heals.

Jochebed

Jochebed gave birth to a son illegally. She hid him as long as she could, but eventually made the difficult choice to place her baby in a basket and hope for the best. That baby was rescued by the pharaoh's daughter and became the great leader of the Israelites long after his adopted mother named him, "Moses."

Jochebed valued motherhood above her own safety, security, or reputation. And God honored Jochebed's mothering heart, for when Pharaoh's daughter needed a wet nurse for Moses, Jochebed got the job. She got to look at that tiny profile while nursing and whisper to him about the God of Israel. The fact that she lived in a culture that was hostile toward mothers was not her legacy.

King Lemuel's Mother

Proverbs 31 is a well-known passage about biblical womanhood, but most of us miss a little snippet of the passage. Verse 1 simply says, "'The words of King Lemuel. An oracle that his mother taught him.'"

Proverbs 31 is really an inside look into a conversation or conversations between a mother and her son. We don't know her name, but we know King Lemuel's mother taught him wisdom. She ripped a page from Eve's motherhood playbook and actively trained her son to please the Lord.

The Proverbs 31 mom shows us what our own legacy can be. I'm sure she changed diapers and made sacrifices and wrestled with unmet expectations. But ultimately, she graced the pages of the Bible because she taught her son about God and righteous living. The words of wisdom she passed on as she mothered became her legacy.

So Go Build Your Wall

In the book of Nehemiah we also find a story with the power to redefine motherhood. Nehemiah was a trusted official under the Persian King Artaxerxes. He was also an Israelite who asked the king to let him gather his people to rebuild the walls of Jerusalem.

The king agreed, so people gathered and the building began. When the enemies of Israel pushed back against the project, pay close attention to how the Israelites defended themselves:

> Therefore I stationed some of the people behind the lowest points of the wall at the exposed places, *posting them by families*, with their swords, spears and bows. After I looked things over, I stood up and said to the nobles, the officials and the rest of the people, "Don't be afraid of them. Remember the Lord, who is great and awesome, and fight for your brothers, your sons and your daughters, your wives and your homes."
>
> When our enemies heard that we were aware of their plot and that God had frustrated it, we all returned to the wall, each to his own work. (Nehemiah 4:13–15 NIV, 1984, emphasis mine)

Instead of using an army of men, Nehemiah urged the people to fight by family. Husbands and wives gathered their children around them and prepared to fight for what mattered. Could they have been victorious any other way? I don't think so. Because they were fighting *for* their families, they were brave enough to stare down their enemies. And because they were fighting *with* their families, they were strong enough to win.

The Israelites continued to work with their families to rebuild the wall. To what end?

"So the wall was finished. . . . And when all our enemies heard of it, all the nations around us were afraid and fell greatly in their own esteem, for they perceived that this work had been accomplished with the help of our God" (6:15–16).

Because the people of Israel fought with their families and for their families, they completed a mighty task that displayed God's glory. Their story reminds me of the battle we are in and the kingdom we are called to build.

The moms from Nehemiah's days encourage us to ask, "What if parenting isn't just about raising good kids but about winning a war? What if you aren't just building a family, but are building a kingdom that will endure?"

THE MOMS FROM Nehemiah's days encourage us to ask, "What if parenting isn't just about raising good kids but about winning a war? What if you aren't just building a family, but are building a kingdom that will endure?"

The builders of the wall join Eve and the other biblical moms in pushing us to think beyond the daily chores of mothering. They remind us that so much more is at stake than what we see in the daily grind of our role.

Their stories remind me of the heroes of faith who are commended in Hebrews 11. The entire chapter applauds people who served God faithfully even when their circumstances were difficult.

That chapter wraps up with these words: "And all these, though commended through their faith, did not receive what was promised, since God had provided something better for us, that apart from us they should not be made perfect" (Hebrews 11:39–40).

They didn't get to see the fruits of their labor, yet they pressed on. They left a legacy of faith even without an immediate payoff. Why? Check out the encouragement in these verses: "Therefore, since we are surrounded by so great a cloud of witnesses, let us also lay aside every weight, and sin which clings so closely, and let us run with endurance the race that is set before us, looking to Jesus, the founder and perfector of our faith, who for the joy that was set before him endured the cross, despising the shame, and is seated at the right hand of the throne of God" (Hebrews 12:1–2).

Listen, moms! You're not just raising kids; you're living your faith. You're not just mothering; you are running a race before many witnesses. You're not on an unclear path; you are to follow in the footsteps of Jesus, who endured more hardship than you ever will. And He endured so you and your children can join Him in heaven at God's right hand.

Mothering has always been hard. The rewards are often difficult to see. But listen to the secret that Eve tells: "*With the help of the Lord* I have brought forth a man" (Genesis 4:1 NIV, emphasis mine).

You can make your mothering count, with the help of the Lord.

The Israelite families knew they weren't just building a wall. Likewise, you're not just building a family; you are building your part of the kingdom. Doing so has the power to strike fear in the hearts of the enemies of God and put His power and glory on full display.

The moms of the Bible didn't measure their success by one

moment, one day, or one feeling. I think they understood better than we do that their work had eternal significance.

Mom, lean in. Listen closely to what Eve is singing over you. Pay close attention to the back-up vocals from Sarah, Bathsheba, Hannah, the Canaanite woman, Jochebed, and the mother of King Lemuel. Let their voices echo through the Hall of Faith and bounce off the walls of Jerusalem. They're saying words you need to hear if you're going to grasp God's plan for your mothering. They are the teachers of the most important lesson you will ever learn about you and your kids.

It's about legacy.

You're having an impact on God's kingdom.

Keep building.

Connecting the Dots

1. Which mom in the Bible do you relate to best? Why?

2. At this stage of parenting, what do you think is your legacy? What do you hope it is by the time your kids have flown the nest and are raising their own baby birds?

3. What is the toughest thing about living your faith in front of your children? The easiest?

4. What are some of the ways your family works together to build walls of faith and unity?

CHAPTER 6:

He Chose a Womb

Motherhood seems to be made up of a million small things. We hold our tiny babies. We fold their little clothes. We lose their itty-bitty shoes in our minivans and their teensy weensy socks in our dryers. We celebrate baby steps and small victories. And some days we can't seem to think past the smallest increments of time—five more minutes of sleep, thirty-second showers, two-minute time-outs.

All of those small things tend to narrow our focus, but the big picture is much, well, bigger.

Nothing is bigger than the gospel. The message that Jesus Christ left heaven, came to earth, and died to rescue us from sin and make a way for us to live with Him for eternity is huge. It's significant. It's complex. It's weighty. The good news of the gospel is very, very big.

Does the big message of the gospel teach us anything about the seemingly small tasks of mothering? Can we learn anything from the big story of Jesus to apply to the little stories we live out with our children?

The New Testament opens with these words: "The book of the genealogy of Jesus Christ, the son of David, the son of Abraham" (Matthew 1:1).

From there, the gospel story unfolds with a long list of birth announcements as the writer traces Jesus' family through forty-two generations. The list includes mothers like Rahab, Ruth, and Bathsheba. Other mothers' names are left off the list, but their role in the bigger story is not lost.

The greatest story ever told begins with a history of parents and families. This set the stage for the arrival of the Messiah.

The genealogies listed in the first verses of Matthew wrap up this way: "And Jacob the father of Joseph the husband of Mary, of whom Jesus was born, who is called Christ" (vv. 16–17).

Suddenly we see her. She's the new mom at the table. At this point Mary probably had more questions than answers about diapers and discipline. She was not a seasoned veteran yet, but her mothering journey has much to teach us.

It's impossible to look at motherhood through the lens of God's Word and not talk about Mary. If any woman in history has been defined by her role as a mother, it's Mary. It's not that Mary herself is sacred, but the circumstances of her family help us see why mothering is such a big deal.

Before she got pregnant, Mary was a simple Hebrew girl who wasn't on anyone's radar screen. Well, that's not exactly true— God's eyes certainly saw her. In fact, He chose her for a monumental mission.

What job title did God give her? Not pastor. Not missionary. Not revolutionary. Nope. God's assignment for His favored one was to be a mom.

"In the sixth month the angel Gabriel was sent from God to a city of Galilee named Nazareth, to a virgin betrothed to a man whose name was Joseph, of the house of David. And the virgin's name was Mary. And he came to her and said, 'Greetings, O favored one, the Lord is with you!' But she was greatly troubled at the saying and tried to discern what sort of greeting this might be. And the angel said to her, 'Do not be afraid, Mary, for you have found favor with God. And behold, you will conceive in your womb and bear a son, and you shall call his name Jesus. He will be great and will be called the Son of the Most High. And the Lord God will give to him the throne of his father David, and he will reign over the house of Jacob forever, and of his kingdom there will be no end." (Luke 1:26–33)

The list of firsts in this passage is rich. It's the first news that the long-awaited Savior was on His way. It's the first time Mary learned she was pregnant and the first time she heard her baby's name. It's the first time we realize the complex and mysterious truth that the King of kings and Lord of lords chose to come to earth just like the rest of us—through a mother's womb.

Not an Ordinary Birth

My doula has delivered hundreds of babies. She says she could ask a mom to write the story of delivering her child fifteen minutes after giving birth and the mom would record every detail. Then she could ask that same mom to write the story fifteen, twenty, or thirty years later and the accounts would be identical. No details would be forgotten, because the experience of bringing children into the world is so powerful that every part of it is burned into our hearts.

Most of us could recite some details of Jesus' birth. We've lived through enough Christmases to remember the stable, the shepherds, and the star. But we don't know the story as Mary does.

If we could talk to Mary, more than two thousand years after she gave birth to the Messiah, she would likely still be able to tell us about every smell in that manger. She'd tell us what Jesus' little head smelled like the first time she kissed it and what she noticed first about the baby King. She would tell us how Joseph helped during painful contractions and pushing. Every color, scent, emotion, and facial expression would be seared into her memory.

Jesus had a spectacular birth. His birth announcements came through a choir of glowing angels (Luke 2:8–21) and a moving star that lured wise men from faraway lands (Matthew 2:1–12). But Mary's role in those historic events was pretty ordinary.

Since the ordinary nature of motherhood often causes us to question its significance, let's consider whether the ordinary or the extraordinary had a greater impact on Jesus' story. The shepherds saw Jesus and then went back to herding sheep. The wise men left their presents at the baby shower and then returned to their own land.

But Mary is woven into every crevice of Jesus' story. From His conception to His death and resurrection, Jesus' mother was a constant player in God's plan to redeem us through the life and death of His Son.

The Ties Jesus Chose

As we examine the gospels, we find that despite Jesus' divinity and Mary's humanity, Jesus and His mother were connected with the same ties that bind us to our children.

In Matthew 2:13, Joseph received instructions to "rise, take the child and his mother, and flee to Egypt." Later Joseph was told, "Rise, take the child and his mother and go to the land of Israel" (Matthew 2:20). So, "he rose and took the child and his mother" (v. 21).

If Jesus was going somewhere, His mother was going with Him. Jesus may be the King of Kings, but His ties to His mother were just like everyone else's. The two of them could not be separated.

Of course we keep our children close to us. We know they need us, and we would never think of moving to foreign lands without them.

But have you ever thought about the fact that in this case, Jesus was the one who chose? Being fully God, Jesus chose to come to earth. He chose to come as an infant, and He chose to be mothered. He chose to be tied to a sinful, inexperienced, inadequate human in this way.

BEING FULLY GOD, Jesus chose to come to earth.
He chose to come as an infant, and He chose to be
mothered. He chose to be tied to a sinful,
inexperienced, inadequate human in this way.

John 1:14 says, "And the Word became flesh and dwelt among us, and we have seen his glory, glory as of the only Son from the Father, full of grace and truth."

Jesus' choice to leave His heavenly garments and take on skin means we serve a God who knows the struggles of this life. And because we know He endured the good, the bad, and the ugly sides of humanity, as Hebrews 4:14–16 points out, we can confidently approach Him. His humanity is a critical part of our relationship with Him. As we look at the accounts of Jesus' life recorded in the Bible, nothing reveals that humanity more than His relationship with His mother.

What does your relationship with your children reveal about God? What bigger story are you telling the world by mothering your children well?

Mary accepted God's call to mother and showed the world that Jesus was a God who intimately knew the complexities of human connection. As a result, we can approach Him. Is it possible that your choices about mothering impact others' willingness to approach God's throne?

Finding Ourselves in Mary's Story

Let's look at the highlight reel and notice how common themes of our mothering experiences are laced throughout the Messiah's story.

In Luke 1:39–56, Mary told Elizabeth about her hopes and fears for motherhood. Elizabeth was also pregnant, and the two gushed and giggled about their unborn babies. I am sure they also shared some nervous laughter about their coming roles. It's the same conversation we have with our mommy friends during play dates or at PTA fund-raisers.

In Luke 2:22, Mary and Joseph presented their baby to the Lord in the temple. Just like we do at baby dedication services and chris-tenings, they officially announced that they would do their best to raise Jesus to know and follow God—and they probably secretly hoped they could be wise and strong enough to follow through.

In Luke 2:33, Joseph and Mary marveled at the amazing things the prophet, Simeon, said about their son.

You've done that, right? Someone spoke about your child's abilities or talents or future, and you marveled at what God was doing in and through your child. From wonder to pride to worry, Mary knew the same emotions of motherhood that we do.

In Luke 2:41–52, Jesus was lost for three days. His parents panicked and then expressed relief when they found Jesus in the temple. And then we see Mary using a mothering tactic most of us have employed. "Mary said, 'Son, why have you treated us so?'" (v. 48).

How do we know Mary was just an ordinary mother? Because we see her laying a guilt trip on her firstborn. It worked about as well on Jesus as it does on our children, another comforting reminder that we are all in the same boat.

Mary was influential in Jesus' first miracle. In John 2:1–12, we read that Jesus and His mother were attending a wedding. The wine had run out, and Mary brought the situation to her son's attention.

"And Jesus said to her, 'Woman, what does this have to do with me? My hour has not yet come'" (v. 4). So what did Mary do? She told the servants to do whatever Jesus asked (v. 5). Just like all moms who know their children's potential to do great things, perhaps Mary gave Jesus a little push to perform miracles.

Mary also faced parenting circumstances that hopefully none of us ever will. She watched as her son was crucified. He endured something unimaginably horrible and her heart must have been torn to shreds, but she did not leave His side, because that was her boy and mommas stay no matter how tough the road gets.

Even when her son was dead, Mary faithfully visited the tomb, and on the third day she was among the first to hear the news her heart longed for, that her son had risen. Forty days later, Mary was at a crossroads that all of us will come to—she had to let her son go for good. She had to rest in the knowledge that He was accomplishing great things and that her years of mothering were not in vain.

Revelation 19:16 tells us that Jesus is the King of kings. So why didn't He come to earth with an entourage? Why did He ditch an earthly throne for a carpenter's bench? Why did He choose to enter our world through the womb of a mother named Mary?

Jesus' choice to come to us through a mother's womb is a huge reminder that motherhood matters. Jesus took on flesh, but He could have come as a fully grown man. Instead He shared the very human experience of being born and cared for by a mother.

JESUS' CHOICE TO come to us through
a mother's womb is a huge reminder
that motherhood matters.

As a man, He may not have walked a mile in our mommy shoes, but He made sure He was not far removed from our experiences as moms.

The list of other lessons that Mary can teach us is long. Her story reminds me that God's favor is shown to me by His choice to allow me to become a mom.

- The "little" things I am doing every day with my children are more important than the noneternal but seemingly big things others are doing.
- Jesus values mothers.
- Extraordinary doesn't always translate to a greater impact than the ordinary. I am influencing my children in big ways by consistently taking care of the small stuff.

These are great lessons, but the point of Mary's story isn't just that motherhood matters. She wasn't chosen to bear Jesus just so she could experience motherhood and we could relate to her and her supernatural Son.

Mary was chosen to mother so that Christ could be born. Christ was born so He could live, and He lived so He could die. He died so He could prove His divinity and conquer our common Enemy by triumphing over the grave. And then He ascended to the throne with the promise that He was preparing a place for us to join Him.

Little things often build into something bigger. That's why we need to remember the gospel when we think about mothering.

Your day may be filled with small tasks for little people. Your time and resources and patience may be in short supply. The rewards of your work as a mom may be difficult to measure in anything but small increments. Focusing on all the little stuff may make you temporarily forget about the big God who paid a huge price to adopt you into His family.

Yes, Jesus chose a womb. But the bigger choice was to make a way to save you from your sin. As you remember that, it has the power to move you from the little things that make mothering tough to the big idea that you are a critical part in the larger story.

Smack dab in the middle of a book on mothering may seem to be a strange place for a gospel presentation, but we need to be reminded of the bigger picture. While the effects of sin permeate our relationships, choices, and days, Jesus died on the cross to give us abundant life (John 10:10). With that in mind, we see that no challenge is too big or too small for us to conquer. If we keep our eyes fixed on our big God while we mother, the little things that overwhelm us get smaller.

Ultimately, Mary's job was much more than just being Jesus' mother. She was the conduit for the transforming power of the gospel.

So are you.

Some days, you may feel you are doing nothing more than pushing a stroller or shuffling a van filled with rowdy boys to Little League, but God's Word reminds us we are running a very big race:

> To the weak I became weak, that I might win the weak. I have become all things to all people, that by all means I might save some. I do it all for the sake of the gospel, that I may share with them in its blessings.
>
> Do you not know that in a race all the runners run, but only one receives the prize? So run that you may obtain it. Every athlete exercises self-control in all things. They do it to receive a perishable wreath, but we an imperishable. (1 Corinthian 9:22–25)

You are doing big things, mom! And you are part of a much bigger story. Refuse to narrow your vision to all the little things and fix your eyes on what Jesus did for you and is doing through you and your children.

{ *More WISE Words* }

A NATIONAL SURVEY conducted by the Search Institute to help determine what factors influenced teens in their faith [says] . . . the most significant religious influence for Christian teens today is . . . Mom.

—MARK HOLMEN[29]

When the little things of mothering feel like they just might swallow you, reach to a big God and ask for the strength to keep running.

Drawing strength for the little things from our big God and His big sacrifice is only one reason why our discussions about motherhood must be peppered with the gospel. Remember that passage in Titus 2: "But as for you, teach what accords with sound doctrine.

... [Older women] are to teach what is good, and so train the young women to love their husbands and children, to be self-controlled, pure, working at home, kind, and submissive to their own husbands, that the word of God may not be reviled" (Titus 2:1, 3–5).

The ins and outs of motherhood need to be taught, and God's Word should be our teacher, but Paul also outlines the stakes when we lose our focus on the biggest tenets of God's truth: "That the word of God may not be reviled."

When we leave God out of our parenting equation, His story gets diluted. When we compartmentalize our lives and forget to apply the good news of the gospel to what we do with our children, God's words lose their grip on our hearts. And when we let the little things of life swallow all of our time, energy, and joy, the gospel message suffers.

WHEN WE LEAVE God out of our parenting equation, His story gets diluted.

What's the biggest lesson we can learn about mothering from a God who chose a womb? Motherhood always plays a part in the much bigger story, and every goldfish cracker dished out, every diaper changed, and every child loved has the power to remind others of Jesus' sacrifice for our sins and His promise of hope, joy, and freedom.

Connecting the Dots

1. Write down all the details you can remember about your little one entering the world.

2. Now think about your own spiritual birth. Describe the time when you welcomed Jesus into your heart.

3. How has motherhood challenged your faith? In what ways has it helped you grow closer to God?

4. Mary was chosen to give birth to our Savior. Why do you think God chose you to be a mother? Hint: you might need to think about this one for a few minutes, it's that deep!

CHAPTER 7:

Blessing or Burden?

In the quest to redefine motherhood as sacred, perhaps the biggest question is, "Are my children a blessing or a burden?"

Obviously, we know the right answer. Our children are a blessing, given to us by a loving God. That's certainly true when they come to us, neatly gift-wrapped in a swaddling blanket after delivery. And it's true when they give us an unexpected cuddle, or when they clean their rooms without being asked, or in the precious silence that comes when they finally fall asleep.

But in general, as we parent each day, do we really see our children as blessings? Or do our actions reveal that we consider them more of a burden?

Motherhood is tough. That's an understatement! Motherhood is like running a marathon uphill in your church shoes (because your toddler took your sneakers in a game of hide-and-seek). When looking at the big picture, being a mom looks great, but navigating among endless dirty diapers, discipline hurdles, potty training, and runny noses can easily choke out the joy of parenting.

{ *More WISE Words* }

"PREGNANCY IS NOT a disease, and children are not a 'health problem'—they are the next generation of Americans."

—CARDINAL DANIEL N. DINARDO, ARCHBISHOP OF GALVESTON—HOUSTON[30]

On top of these challenges we must listen to our culture's subtle—and blatant—suggestions that children are cute, but life would be easier without them.

We may be moms, but we certainly aren't supposed to like it. Want proof? Just tell someone you're getting a minivan. They will laugh. They will feel sorry for you. They will act as if this is trading all passion, freedom, and fun for seven seats, cruise control, and built-in DVD players.

Want another test? Wear mom jeans. Yes, those jeans that scream, "I am a mom; my life as an attractive, valuable woman is officially over."

Every makeover show holds up mom jeans as the ultimate fashion faux pas. You may be a mom, but you'd better not look like one.

You don't want everyone knowing about the little people who have sucked all of the fun, glamour, and excitement from your life.

God's Word teaches a very different truth. Letting the truth help you make the choice—and it is a choice!—to see your children as a blessing can change your role as a mom.

I love being a mom, but I haven't always felt this way. Many days the tasks of mothering seem so cumbersome that I feel weighed down. I don't say, "My children are such a burden!" But those feelings are revealed in my words and actions:

- When I regularly lose my cool with my kids and justify it by pointing the finger back at them.
- When I gripe about being up all night, the latest troubling behavior I have to retrain, or the fact that I can't even go to the bathroom alone.
- When I use the word "overwhelmed" to describe my life more often than I use words like "blessed, happy, or fulfilling."
- When my husband comes in the door and I announce I am "off duty" because I cannot handle one more minute with the kids.
- When I let my mind dwell on all the bummers that come with children instead of choosing to think about the blessings only motherhood can give.

I don't sound the burden alarm all the time. You probably don't either. At times we clearly let our kids know we're tickled they're ours. But I miss the mark in this area more often than I'd like.

How about you? Our behavior *toward* our children and our

conversations *about* our children send a message in one of two directions. Either we communicate that our children are a blessing, or that they are a burden.

Instead of dissecting our every move to see how we fare on the blessing or burden scale, I think it is most helpful to uncover God's answer to this fundamental question. When it comes to children, where does He stand?

One of the clearest answers to this question is in Psalms 127 and 128. As we unpack these verses, we discover that when we see our children as a burden even for a moment, we've got it all wrong.

"Unless the Lord builds the house, those who build it labor in vain. Unless the Lord watches over the city, the watchman stays awake in vain. It is in vain that you rise up early and go late to rest, eating the bread of anxious toil; for he gives to his beloved sleep" (Psalm 127:1–2).

There's enough mom language in these verses to make me take notice. Labor, keeping watch, anxiousness, late nights, and early mornings are inevitable components of our mom worlds. The psalmist revealed that if the Lord is not in the work we do, including parenting, we are laboring in vain. If you watch your children solely out of duty or if you feel the entire weight of parenting rests on you, your tired eyes are for nothing.

Dig deep, momma, and ask this question: If these verses are true, if the Lord *is* involved in your job as a mom, if He really is the one building your house and keeping watch over your family, isn't there reason for joy?

Psalm 16:11 says, "You make known to me the path of life; in your presence there is fullness of joy; at your right hand are pleasures forevermore."

The charge in Colossians 1:10–12 certainly applies to our mission as moms: "Walk in a manner worthy of the Lord, fully pleasing to him, bearing fruit in every good work and increasing in the knowledge of God. May you be strengthened with all power, according to his glorious might, for all endurance and patience with joy, giving thanks to the Father, who has qualified you to share in the inheritance of the saints in light."

No matter how many challenges we face, we can be strengthened with God's power. We don't have to do it all in our own strength. And how do these verses urge us to respond to this promise? With patience, joy, and thanksgiving.

Since God is with us, we have reason to be joyful about, and toward, our children. What a difference it would make if we each decided to shift from being a burdened mom to being a joyful one!

As we keep reading Psalm 127:3–5, we uncover God's clear answer to the burden-or-blessing question: "Behold, children are a heritage from the Lord, the fruit of the womb a reward. Like arrows in the hand of a warrior are the children of one's youth. Blessed is the man who fills his quiver with them! He shall not be put to shame when he speaks with his enemies in the gate."

God sees children as a heritage, a reward, ammunition for a battle, much like arrows in the hands of a warrior (if you've forgotten where the battle is, reread chapter 2), a blessing, and a source of respect, even among our enemies. This passage doesn't reveal even a hint of burden. God doesn't gripe about the challenges of parenting or fixate on ways children try us. Instead, His stance is that children are a blessing. Period.

Psalm 128 backs this up.

Blessed is everyone who fears the Lord, who walks in his ways! You shall eat the fruit of the labor of your hands; you shall be blessed, and it shall be well with you. Your wife will be like a fruitful vine within your house; your children will be like olive shoots around your table.

Behold, thus shall the man be blessed who fears the Lord." (vv. 1–4)

What word is used repeatedly in these verses? Blessed. If we fear the Lord we are blessed. If we walk in His ways, we are blessed. A wife who bears children is a blessing. And those children are like a blessing of olive shoots.

Since most of us get our olives from the can, I consulted my favorite gardening expert, Google, to find out what's so great about a bunch of olive shoots.

I found that when you look at most olive trees, you see many baby tree shoots growing out of the root system around the tree. Having all of that new life so close to the trunk is good. Though the mother tree has to share her soil, her water, and her personal space, those little olive shoots don't rob the tree of its nutrients, steal all of its water, or suck the mother tree dry. The mature olive tree becomes surrounded by a band of healthy successors. It's an image of new life, growth, and productivity that is a blessing—not a drag.

And God's Word says more! In Genesis 33:5, Jacob describes his children as a gracious gift from God. Titus 2:3–5 reminds us that the way we treat our children is tied to the way others see God's Word, and that loving them is a choice we should make as believing women. The children of the Proverbs 31 woman adored her and saw her as blessed (Proverbs 31:28). Jesus knew children were a worthy investment of His time (Matthew 19:13).

Nearly every reference to children in the Bible shows that God considers them a blessing, not a curse.

These biblical points look nice in cross-stitch, but are difficult to remember when the daily strain of parenting piles on our shoulders. When we forget our children are gifts, we get discouraged, overwhelmed, and cranky.

That's the state I was in most of the time during my early years as a mom. And I still have that state of mind at times. But when my shoulders start to sag, I can choose to believe what God says about my kiddos. This is an area where I need to grab onto God's truth and hold on for dear life.

WHEN MY SHOULDERS start to sag, I can choose to believe what God says about my kiddos.

Blessings and Burdens Are in Cahoots

To help us see our children as less of a burden, let's redefine the word *blessing*. Merriam-Webster defines a blessing as "a thing conducive to happiness or welfare."[31]

When my kids throw a tantrum (usually in front of a crowd at church), that isn't exactly conducive to my happiness. When I'd rather sleep in but must get up and dish out Cheerios, it might not promote my general welfare. When cleaning the garage with my husband counts as a date because it's the only way we can snag time alone together, I may not feel warm fuzzies. But that doesn't mean I'm not blessed.

And here's a radical thought: perhaps blessings and burdens are not mutually exclusive. Just because something is hard or cumbersome, doesn't mean it's not a blessing.

BLESSINGS AND BURDENS are not mutually exclusive. Just because something is hard or cumbersome, doesn't mean it's not a blessing.

James understood this when he wrote, "Count it all joy, my brothers, when you meet trials of various kinds" (James 1:2).

Motherhood may include many trials, but that doesn't mean you aren't blessed. We think being blessed means we feel happy, our life is easy, and everything is smooth sailing. But we are actually blessed when we are doing kingdom work and when our circumstances make us more like Jesus and press us into a closer relationship with Him.

Children are a blessing in the traditional sense. Amid all of the work and chaos are those faces we love so much it feels as if our hearts might burst. But we also have to fix our eyes on the more intangible ways they are a blessing.

Think about the ways that your children don't feel like a blessing, and then force yourself to flip your circumstances over and see the other side of the coin.

The burdens and blessings of motherhood are in constant flux from that moment we bring our babies home. There are always noses to wipe, tantrums to referee, and globs of toothpaste to wipe. Sure, those things look like a burden at first glance. But without those burdens you could never know the blessings of a house filled with laughter, a faded flower picked and delivered just for you, or the feel of a chubby hand slipped inside yours. The weight of the emotional and physical toll of mothering may feel heavy at times, but without it you could never know the joy that comes from the unconditional love that children offer so freely.

The burdens of motherhood are more like little geodes. They are rough to touch and heavy to carry at times, but do some digging and you're bound to discover breathtaking treasure. Your children may stretch, try, and challenge you, but they are ultimately not a burden. They are the geodes God has entrusted to you and if you're willing to mine they are bound to return to you blessings you never knew to look for.

Burden-proofing Your Child's Heart

While I was researching how to baby-proof my home, I read that I should get down on all fours and look at the house from their level. Besides discovering a few treasures that had lived under the furniture for months, I also saw dangers that lurked at the same height as little hands, fingers, and toes.

When we take a second look at the way we act toward and talk about our kids, we see ourselves through their eyes. It's alarming to see the dangers caused by any sense that our children are a burden. Every sharp word, gripe session, complaint, and mommy meltdown suddenly seems like a source of real danger.

So go on, hunker down, and see the hazards of your subtle complaints. See the damage that your sighs and mutterings can do to little hearts. If you look at your behavior through their eyes, do your children feel celebrated? Treasured? As something good? Or might they feel like a burden?

There is real danger for your children in feeling unwanted, even if only occasionally. It is very painful for them to feel that someone—especially someone they love as much as their mom— is sad, tired, stressed out, and overwhelmed, because they have needs they cannot yet meet on their own.

THERE IS REAL danger for your children in feeling unwanted, even if only occasionally. It's very painful for them to feel someone they love as much as their mom is sad, tired, stressed out, and overwhelmed, because they have needs they cannot yet meet on their own.

If you see some danger zones, let that motivate you to do what it takes to burden-proof your children's hearts.

This exercise of asking the blessing/burden question through the eyes of her young daughters helped writer Sheri Prescott see the joy of motherhood.

"I love to watch my daughters play house with their baby dolls," she writes. "They so lovingly change their little outfits; wrapping them carefully in soft blankets and singing softly as they lay their baby in its wooden cradle. They love to set them in tiny strollers and zoom all over the house. They pretend to nurse their bundles of joy and then feed them gooey pretend baby food with a plastic spoon. Motherhood looks so peaceful and beautiful to a young girl."

This may seem simplistic. Certainly little girls mothering their baby dolls don't have to deal with sibling rivalry or back talk. But their love for the job of "mommy" is similar to the childlike faith Jesus found so enduring. Being a mom is exciting to them because their eyes see the peaks of parenting for what they really are—joyous!

Prescott continues, "Sure, there will be hard days and *harder* days, but focus on the simple, good things. . . . Pretend you are a little girl, full of expectation and dreams of motherhood. Float with your babes around the room and zoom around the neighborhood with your real stroller. May we start to look at motherhood through the innocent, fresh eyes of a young girl playing house. Because to them, motherhood is a joy. And, I think, that's just what our Heavenly Father wants motherhood to be."[32]

God's plan is for children to be a blessing and for mothering to be a joy. That doesn't mean it's easy, but Easy Street rarely leads to anywhere truly fulfilling anyway. Intentionally set your feet on a different path—the path of choosing to believe God's truth about children. This path leads to righteousness, to happier children and husbands, to calmer mommies, to families the world will notice, and ultimately, to blessing.

Practically speaking, how do you make yourself feel blessed in the midst of your to-do list, exhaustion, and messy house?

Act out joy.

JOY ISN'T THE same as slapping a smile on your face and trying to convince yourself everything is peachy. Joy is choosing to live like all is well—and all will be well because God is with you in all circumstances.

Dispense an insane number of hugs and kisses. Tell your children they are a blessing so often they roll their eyes. Pull out baby books and relive the joy of meeting your children for the first time. Hang out with friends who think of motherhood as an honor. Create a Kid's Day tradition to celebrate your kids. Change the way you respond to your kids and let your feelings catch up.

The bottom line: delighting in our children is a choice. It's a mothering lesson I wish I'd learned sooner, but one I remind myself of every time parenting gets hairy.

What delights you about your kids? What can you do to hold tightly to God's truth about them today?

If you are still having trouble flipping the joy switch, consider that joy might be exactly what you need to keep mothering. Joy isn't the same as slapping a smile on your face and trying to convince yourself everything is peachy. Joy is choosing to live like all is well—and all will be well because God is with you in all circumstances. When it comes to motherhood, joy is less like an emotion and more like fuel for the long journey ahead.

Remember Nehemiah? He already taught us to have a kingdom mind-set about parenting. But he also gives advice about how to face the challenges that come with the territory: "Do not be grieved, for the joy of the Lord is your strength" (Nehemiah 8:10).

Why should you choose to live as if you are blessed? Why should you act out joy even when you're cranky and need an uninterrupted shower?

Because joy is a source of strength.

Paul knew this truth. He knew that just because the going was tough didn't mean he wasn't blessed. He faced afflictions we never will, yet he told the Corinthian congregation, "In all our affliction, I am overflowing with joy" (2 Corinthians 7:4).

Whether or not your children are a blessing or a burden has little to do with them. No doubt they'll put you through the ringer. They'll push your buttons, stretch your body, and wear you slick.

But God's Word is clear: Your children are a gift from God.

In light of that truth, how should you respond and where can you turn to for strength—pure joy!

Connecting the Dots

1. List the burdens you face in mothering.

2. Now, list two blessings of mothering for each burden you've listed. Go ahead—you can do it!

3. Look at your relationship with your children from their child's-eye view. If they were honest and knew how to express themselves, do you think they'd consider themselves burdens to you or blessings? Why?

4. What are some of the things you can do to help your children know they are blessings? You might make a list and post it somewhere to remind yourself to work on this.

5. How can you encourage your children to know they are a blessing to God, too? What are some specific things you can do?

CHAPTER 8:

Ministry v. Mundane

Imagine we're at a commissioning service.
One by one, brave, devoted Christians accept the call to ministry
God has placed on their lives.

"I feel called to be a pastor," one says.

"I feel called to be a missionary overseas."

"I feel called to student ministry."

We'd applaud. We'd pray. We'd drop a check in the offering
plate.

But what if a young woman stood and said, "I feel called to be
a mom."

How would we react? What support would we feel challenged
to give? Would we have the same sense that her assignment was
straight from God?

Somehow I doubt it.

Our collective vision of what it means to be an ambassador for
the gospel seems to have gotten a little skewed. Certainly those who

minister to lost people in Africa or pastor churches in Ohio are doing significant works for God. But mission fields exist that don't require seminary degrees, pulpits, or financial backing by the International Mission Board.

As a Christian mom who may be tied to your home, you may be easily discouraged. It may seem your work doesn't matter much or that "out there" is where the real front lines are in the battle to make Jesus known.

Probably no one is asking you for a PowerPoint presentation about being a mom. You may not be on anyone's missionary prayer list or ministry bulletin board.

But that doesn't mean you're not a missionary.

Motherhood is common. It happens in the homes of many Christian families and doesn't offer much glamour, excitement, or novelty. It's easy to assume that because what we are doing is familiar, we are the least valuable part of the church.

But God doesn't see it that way. And we need to remember the sacredness of what we are doing as we mother.

IT'S EASY TO assume that because what we are doing is familiar, we are the least valuable part of the church. But God doesn't see it that way.

A Mom's Role in the Body

God has always been in the business of using His people to do great things for the kingdom. But His vision has never been that pastors, preachers, and vocational missionaries have all the important jobs in Christendom while the rest of us pine for kingdom work beyond our homes.

In 1 Corinthians 12:14–25, we see a better vision of the church and our place in it. "For the body does not consist of one member but of many. If the foot should say, 'Because I am not a hand, I do not belong to the body,' that would not make it any less a part of the body. And if the ear should say, 'Because I am not an eye, I do not belong to the body,' that would not make it any less a part of the body. If the whole body were an eye, where would be the sense of hearing? . . . The eye cannot say to the hand, 'I have no need of you,' nor again the head to the feet, 'I have no need of you.' On the contrary, the parts of the body that seem to be weaker are indispensable." (v. 14–17; 21–22)

For now you may only be the hands that dish out macaroni and cheese or the ears that listen to stories of who won the foursquare battle. Your job in the church at this moment may be as the mouth that teaches the Golden Rule to three little ones instead of to an orphanage. But the smallness of those tasks does not mean you're not a key player in what God is doing in and through the church.

My wise husband sees this reality more clearly than I do. One day he sent me this e-mail, with a picture of our younger son, Noble.

In case you were wondering why you work so hard, why you hit the ground running, and why each day is full of tasks that seem to never completely get done . . . Here is a photo of why you do it. You do it to make his life better. You do it to show him what a life spent for Jesus looks like. You do it so he knows Jesus is more important than he is—but nothing else is. You do it so he can learn important things and avoid learning things he doesn't need to. You do it for me, you do it for Noble, you do it for Eli, and you do it for Jesus. I'm proud of you.

{ *More WISE Words* }

HOW CAN IT be a large career to tell other people's children about the Rule of Three, and a small career to tell one's own children about the universe? How can it be broad to be the same thing to everyone, and narrow to be everything to someone? No; a woman's function is laborious, but because it is gigantic; not because it is minute.

—G. K. CHESTERTON[33]

God used these words to remind me that while my calling may look small, the potential ministry impact is very big. It's hard to see in the thick of life, but if you'll let Him, God will take your small mom offerings and transform them to show others who He is.

Learning to Multiply with Mom Math

God has always used small offerings for big things. Remember how Jesus fed the five thousand with five barley loaves and two fish. That miracle was significant enough to be recorded in all four gospels (Matthew 14:13–21; Mark 6:32–44; Luke 9:10–17; John 6:1–14). It's a story big enough to be taught in every Sunday school class.

Where did those loaves and fish come from anyway? In John 6:9, we read Andrew's words to Jesus, "There is a boy here who has five barley loaves and two fish, but what are they for so many?"

Excuse me while I make an assumption—a momma packed that lunch. Can't you just hear that morning conversation?

Boy: Mom, I'm going to hear the Messiah.

Mom: Wait a minute; let me pack you a snack.

Boy: Aw Mom, I'll be fine!

But that mom knew her boy would have a hard time listening on an empty stomach. So I imagine she packed a snack, dropped in a napkin and a note that said, "I love you," and sent him on his way.

That mom didn't get any props for her effort. But that doesn't mean God didn't use it.

Let's trace the journey of that little lunch. Mom packed the lunch. Boy carried the lunch. Disciples noticed the lunch. Jesus blessed and multiplied the lunch. More than five thousand people ate the lunch. And millions know that Jesus is God because the story of this miracle has been told for thousands of years.

That's how mom math works in the kingdom.

What you're doing might seem small. Little mouths to feed. Little squabbles to referee. Little house to clean. But God multiplies your efforts. Your small tasks point to a very big God if you are determined to do it all for His glory.

Just as our definitions of blessing and burden have gotten jumbled, so have our concepts of big and small stuff for the kingdom. If a woman surrendered her life to share Bible stories with children in unreached people groups overseas, we would consider that big, and rightfully so.

But your children are also an unreached people group. They don't come into the world with a knowledge and heart for God. It's your job to teach them, and it's a big job. It's big in the sense that it demands much of you, but it is also big in the sense that it matters a great deal.

IF A WOMAN surrendered her life to share
Bible stories with children in unreached people
groups overseas, we would consider that big,
and rightfully so. But your children are also
an unreached people group.

Step back and look at the inevitable ripple effect you are putting into motion. Your kids will probably someday have children of their own. How many future families are represented by the faces you wake up to? How will the impact of your work be multiplied in the lives of your children's children?

Here's a wide-angle shot of that thought: "A woman who has two children and whose children each produce two children for ten generations will by the tenth generation have 1,024 offspring. But a woman who has four children and whose children each have four children will by the tenth generation have 1,048,448 descendents!"[34]

Being directly connected to between one thousand and one million Christians is no small thing!

That's how mom math works. You take seriously your role to minister, to shepherd, and to shape your little brood, and God multiplies it for generations to come.

Keep widening your lens and consider how many people will hear the message of Christ if you teach your children to live the Great Commission. How many other moms would be challenged to live Christ-centered parenting if they saw you doing it so well and with joy. How many husbands and children are connected to those moms?

I hope you get the sense that as a mission-focused mom, your job is not small or insignificant. As a colaborer in the trenches of motherhood, I want to nudge you to embrace the radical sentiment that you've been called to something gigantic.

As you look back on these missionary years, you'll see the richness. When your children are grown and serving Christ, you'll know your efforts had value.

But my challenge to you is to see the finish line while you are still running the marathon. Choose to see motherhood in panorama, as your corner of the world where the gospel must be preached.

And here's a flipside.

What if, for now, you are your child's mission field? What if all the ways they challenge you are designed to teach you about your own fleshly heart and sinful tendencies—and thus remind you of your own desperate need for a Savior? What if God has sent them to disciple you, pray for you, and springboard you toward greater sanctification?

Could their acts of disobedience remind you of the ugliness of your own disobedience toward God? What if your children are the way God can show you the biblical truth that discipline is tied to love and is the only way you can see that you serve a good Father?

If your role is to point your children to Christ, and their role is to make you more like Him, you are working together on an important mission indeed.

Let's think back to that commissioning service. In light of what God's Word teaches about our vital role in the body, I hope we would react differently if a mom decided to stand and accept God's calling to motherhood.

We would applaud and support her because we know that being a mom is high, holy, and a worthy investment of the spiritual gifts and opportunities we have been entrusted with.

In fact, I hope you would be that woman. And if we were gathered together around a bonfire or pulpit, I hope that each of us would stand and surrender our mothering journey to Christ and commit to live as if what we are doing is ministry, because it is.

With that image, I want to commission you into Christian service as a mother. When the road gets tough, when you're stressed, or bored, or going cross-eyed from a close-up view of what you're doing, remember that you've been sent to a mission field and that your children are the people God has called you to serve and teach about Him. When the job feels mundane, or underappreciated, pack a little lunch of your time, efforts, and abilities and ask God to multiply it.

With that little offering in mind, I send you out, mom, with a commissioning prayer adapted from *The Book of Common Prayer*. These words were originally written to send Christian laborers into the field. The mission field is your home. Your mission focus is your children. The reward for your mission is mighty.

May the Holy Spirit guide and strengthen you, that in this, and in all things, you may do God's will in the service of the kingdom of His Christ. Amen.

In the name of this congregation of mothers, I commend you to this work, and pledge you our prayers, encouragement, and support.

Let us pray.

Almighty God, look with favor on this mom who has now reaffirmed her commitment to follow Christ and to serve in His name. Give her courage, patience, and vision and strengthen us all in our Christian vocation of witness to the world, and of service to others; through Jesus Christ our Lord. Amen.[35]

Connecting the Dots

1. What is your definition of ministry? List five people you feel have ministries, and what kind of ministries they have.

2. In what ways do you feel mothering is a ministry?

3. How would your daily mind-set change if you truly felt called and ordained by God to have a ministry to your children?

4. In what ways are you "Jesus in the flesh" to your kiddos?

CHAPTER 9:
No Mom Alone

A couple of days after we brought Noble home from the hospital, I was nearly overwhelmed by a wave of postpartum depression. One minute I was sitting on the floor folding tiny clothes, and the next minute I felt as if a dark cloud had enveloped me.

For several weeks I wavered between joy over the new life and intense sadness. At times I felt so overcome by fear, anxiety, and sorrow that I wanted to hop in my minivan, start driving, and never look back.

If you've ever wrestled with postpartum depression, you know the combination of hormones, sleep deprivation, and adjustment to this major life change can mess up your mind.

I was knocked off guard by the level of emotions I felt. And I had no idea how to talk about what I was facing. I couldn't tell my husband that I was fantasizing about hopping in the car and leaving him with two children.

I tried to tell my doctor, but I couldn't admit how scary and dark my world had become. I wouldn't reach out to my church leadership. I assumed I should simply trust God more or read my Bible more. I wrongly assumed that if I opened up to someone at church, that person would see my struggle as an indicator of gaping holes in my faith.

I had been attending a MOPS (Mothers of Preschoolers) group with my toddler. Until Noble was born, MOPS was just a fun excuse to get out of the house, but in the wake of postpartum depression, those moms became my lifeline.

During one MOPS meeting we were sharing prayer requests—safe things to share like a relative's surgery or needs of missionaries. Just as everyone bowed to pray, the levy broke in my heart. I said, "I don't love my husband anymore."

That wasn't true, of course. But postpartum depression combined with sleep deprivation can be a real mind bender, and I couldn't see beyond the hurricane of emotions swirling inside me.

How did those moms respond to my alarming confession? They circled the wagons. They gathered around me and cried over me. They shared their own stories about adjusting to life after a new baby. They were honest about their own feelings toward their husbands and children.

At that moment, when my honesty led to their transparency, I started to see the light at the end of the tunnel.

And then they brought casseroles. For three weeks, they brought us food every night. They didn't just drop off the lasagna and race out the door. They sat in my living room. They asked how I was doing and listened. They prayed with me and for me. They called. They texted. They e-mailed. They made sure I was putting one foot in front of the other.

They breathed life into me.

When the worst had passed, they still let me know I could call them any time the dark clouds rolled in.

I am so thankful I had a community of moms when my mothering journey got rocky. Only in the nest surrounded by other momma birds, did I feel brave enough to say, "I'm struggling." Those moms saved my sanity, they may have saved my marriage, and they let me borrow their strength and wisdom so I could press on.

We need each other, moms. As Christian women, we must find ways to connect with each other and create a support system. Certainly we can find self-help books, mom chat rooms, and community groups to support moms. But those self-help methods are ultimately fruitless if they don't teach mothering tied to your identity and calling from Christ.

Remember Psalm 127:1–2: "Unless the Lord builds the house, those who build it labor in vain. Unless the Lord watches over the city, the watchman stays awake in vain. It is in vain that you rise up early and go late to rest, eating the bread of anxious toil; for he gives to his beloved sleep."

For our mothering efforts to produce eternal fruit, God must be involved. So it seems obvious that the primary job of discipling, equipping, and encouraging moms should fall squarely on the church's shoulders.

To better understand how the church should respond to mothers, we need to ask a big question: Why did God create the church? What's her purpose?

Some of the best answers come from examining the first Christian churches in the book of Acts. In Acts 2:42–47, we find the members of the first church studying biblical teaching, praying together, and celebrating God-given victories with each other. According to Acts 11:26, the church is intended to be a place where

God's truth is taught. In Acts 16:5, we find that the church is a place where the Christian's faith is strengthened and that the church is then used as a vehicle to spread Christ's message.

As Paul taught the early Corinthian church, God has given us the ministry of reconciliation (2 Corinthians 5:17–20). Who are we to be reconciling? The world and Christ. We are ambassadors to those who do not know Christ and to those who need to know Him more.

THE PROMISES OF God spoken by other moms help us persevere, provide strength for gospel-centered mothering, and offer a safety net for when motherhood puts us in a free fall.

The reason for Christian community is to proclaim the good news. Therefore a loving, gospel-saturated community is God's plan to shore up our own hearts and to draw others toward the hope only found in Jesus.

Many times since I have become a mother, the church has been the hands and feet of Jesus in my life, faithfully living out Jesus' instructions to His followers in Matthew 25:36–40.

At times, I've desperately needed the prayers and encouragement of other moms to snap me out of my amnesia about Jesus' promises. If I didn't have other moms to say, "Yep, that's normal" or "This too shall pass" or to encourage me to turn to Jesus when mothering gets tough, I would have been eaten up with worry.

The promises of God spoken by other moms help us persevere, provide strength for gospel-centered mothering, and offer a safety net for when motherhood puts us in a free fall.

Christians are to intentionally create communities that honor what God loves, and we are to disciple others to live like Jesus at every stage of the journey. We've seen God's heart for mothers and children throughout His Word. As a church, if we really want to honor what's close to God's heart, we will support mothers and teach them to parent in a way that exalts Christ.

Now that the battle is obvious, the stakes are clear, and God's truth about motherhood has been laid out, we have a big question to answer: What is God calling us, the church, to do to minister to moms?

The Power of Sisterhood

Certainly, pastors can preach about motherhood; Sunday school teachers can teach about it; and the church can voice support for the hard work Christian moms do. But the real strength and courage necessary to mother are found in the unique bonds of Christian sisterhood.

Women meeting with women creates a potent combination. That's why Paul charged older women to disciple young moms and wives in Titus 2:3–5.

Paul knew the power of moms connecting with other moms. But in the days when Paul wrote these words to Pastor Titus, this formula of older women mentoring younger women happened more naturally than it does today. Mothers, daughters, and grandmothers usually lived near each other or in the same house. This teaching probably occurred around the dining room table or during the course of daily tasks.

Today, most young mothers do not live with or near mothers or grandmothers, so generational mentoring isn't as common. We have to intentionally tap into the power of Christian sisterhood. The church can fill the gaps caused by geography and scheduling, and equip moms to lovingly raise their children for Christ.

Maybe a thriving moms' group at your church already connects moms. How can you get involved? How can you hitch your cart to those women to maximize their wisdom, strength, and encouragement?

{ *More WISE Words* }

"I WAS NAKED and you clothed me, I was sick and you visited me, I was in prison and you came to me." Then the righteous will answer him, saying, "Lord, when did we see you hungry and feed you, or thirsty and give you drink? And when did we see you a stranger and welcome you, or naked and clothe you? And when did we see you sick or in prison and visit you?" And the King will answer them, "Truly, I say to

you, as you did it to one of the least of these
my brothers, you did it to me."

—MATTHEW 25:36–40

If your church doesn't have an organized offensive to disciple and encourage moms, dream with me for a moment. How can your church create a Christian sisterhood that could transform moms and families?

You might think, "I can't even manage to brush my teeth every day or keep the laundry at bay, and now you want me to launch a moms' ministry?"

Motherhood is demanding, and most of us are juggling a million tasks, but if we won't reach out to other moms and encourage our churches to get involved in the battle to preserve God's high and holy calling for mothers, no one will.

I know because I tried to pass the buck in my own church. I tried to persuade staff members and other women to start a ministry to moms. They just looked at me sweetly and said, "Bless your heart," which is Christian code for, "Not on your life."

So I eventually launched a moms' group. It wasn't easy. It required my resources, energy, and patience—already in short supply. But I am so glad I didn't shirk my responsibilities to equip other moms. The results have transformed us all.

Our church's moms' ministry looks like a small group of women who meet once a month to drink coffee out of fancy cups and talk about mothering.

In your church, perhaps a moms' ministry will look like a big group of women who enjoy programmed meetings. Maybe it will be three moms who have weekly play dates. Or maybe it's a Sunday school class focused on studying God's truth for moms.

The shape and size of your group doesn't matter, but it does matter that your church is intentional about being ambassadors for Christ to the moms in your community.

You've now come face-to-face with God's heart for mothers, the challenges mommas face in our antichild climate, and the huge impact that moms determined to see motherhood as a mission field can have.

Now that the truth has been laid out for you, I hope you feel motivated to let it shape the happenings in your own home, and to "pay it forward" to other moms.

If so, here are five easy steps you can take to get started.

1. Pray.

That may seem to be the ultimate Christian cliché, but don't start any ministry without consulting God. He may plan to use you to start a mom ministry—or He may just plan for you to simply get to know the struggling mom across the street. He may have a vision for you to mentor a small group of Christian women, or He may want you to mentor a group of moms at a homeless shelter.

2. Talk to your pastor.

Schedule a time to tell your pastor what God is teaching you about motherhood. Be careful not to attack your pastor for all of the things the church isn't doing for mothers. Instead, work together to find ways to encourage and equip moms, with the goal of strengthening Christian families.

3. Recruit mentor moms.

The formula in Titus 2:3–5 is relatively simple—older women are to teach and younger women are to learn. Find some women who have paid a few motherhood dues and have a gospel-centered mothering approach and ask them to dream with you about how to pass on what they've learned to other moms.

4. Pray.

Did I say that already? I meant it. Pray about how your church can meet the unique needs of moms. But I already know one of the biggest needs of moms—prayer. We moms need to pray together and for each other.

Remember the stakes: Raising the next generation of people who will either follow or abandon the truth about God. If that's really what's on the line, how motivated do you think the Enemy is to destroy Christian mothers and families?

Remember the church in Acts? They were serious about prayer. Acts 1:14 (NIV) says, "They all joined together constantly in prayer."

Could they have prayed individually in the privacy of their homes? Certainly. That probably would have been a safer option, considering the persecution they faced. But they met and prayed together, because they knew the strength they could find by doing so.

Matthew 18:19–20 gives this bold promise: "If two of you agree on earth about anything they ask, it will be done for them by my Father in heaven. For where two or three are gathered in my name, there am I among them."

Clearly, we find power in praying together!

If you don't take another step to reach out to moms, take this one. Find some moms in your church and start praying together. For great resources, check out Moms in Touch International at momsintouch.org.

5. Connect online.

We have a website loaded with help as moms take practical steps to embrace motherhood as sacred. For more information about how to start a moms' group, encouragement, and the chance to connect with other moms who want to turn the tide, check us out at www.beyondbathtime.com.

Imagine your church in twenty-five years. The babies in the nursery will be college graduates. The students in the youth group will have children. The kids who learn the basics of faith at vacation Bible school may be spreading that truth as ministers, missionaries, or missional moms. With that perspective, I hope you will adopt the mantra that MOPS used several years ago: "No mom alone!"

Moms, we need each other. We need support when our energy, resources, and patience are sagging. We need encouragement to treat motherhood as a mission field. We need other moms to pray with and for us. We need to recognize that sisterhood is powerful and to live out God's truth even when it's countercultural. As a church and as individuals, we need to accept responsibility to teach women to live like Christ.

When reaching out to other moms feels like one more thing on my to-do list, I remember those moms who loved me through my darkest days. Because of them, I am a better mother. In many ways, their words, prayers, and casseroles will be passed down for generations to come.

WHEN REACHING OUT to other moms feels like one more thing on my to-do list, I remember those moms who loved me through my darkest days.

That's how mom math works in the kingdom. Little words become lifelines. Little prayers move mountains of laundry, fear, and hurt. What little thing can you do for another mom today to strengthen her to live that calling God has placed on her life?

"Pay careful attention to yourselves and to all the flock, in which the Holy Spirit has made you overseers, to care for the church of God, which he obtained with his own blood" (Acts 20:28).

Connecting the Dots

1. Write about a time motherhood set your emotions in a whirl.

2. Who has been most supportive to you in your mothering journey? What are some of the ways this person has helped you?

3. How would you like to see the church support moms better?

4. As part of the church, how can you support moms better? What can you do to help mothers connect?

5. What advice would you, as a more experienced mom, give to a new mother? List three things.

CHAPTER 10:

A New Breed of Hero

I've always adored Wonder Woman. With enviable powers such as superhuman strength, amazing speed, and unbelievable stamina, she's unstoppable. Wonder Woman always knows how to take out the bad guys, and she can do it all in a killer pair of red boots. She's impressive and glamorous, and many days I want to be just like her.

But I will never be Wonder Woman. I don't have superhuman strength. If motherhood has taught me anything, it is how often my strength fails.

I don't have amazing speed anymore. I have to fight the temptation to think of my children as speed bumps, slowing me down.

I certainly don't have unbelievable stamina. Most days I collapse on the couch long before the dishes get done, the toys get picked up, or my husband gets any attention.

The "bad guys" my children face seem too numerous for me to battle. From flu viruses to learning hurdles to the Enemy who seeks to "kill and destroy" our family (John 10:10), I know I can't keep all the danger at bay.

And as far as the boots go . . . I feel a little silly wearing knee-high red boots to story time at the library or hide-and-seek at the park.

I may not be a superstar who will ever be drawn into a comic strip, but that doesn't mean I'm not a hero. In fact, in the real world, moms are the heroines.

Hidden Sources of Strength

When we look at Christian history, we find many superheroes of the faith. Consider the Wesley brothers, John and Charles. John was an eighteenth-century English preacher and theologian credited with an evangelistic revival that emphasized serving others and spreading the good news. Many came to know Christ through Wesley's preaching, and he eventually ignited a movement that became the Methodist Church.

John's brother Charles also played a key role in the Methodist revival. You may not know much about Charles, but I am sure you have sung hymns he wrote, including "Christ the Lord Is Risen Today" and "Hark! The Herald Angels Sing."

John and Charles Wesley are heroes of the Christian faith. Their efforts have affected millions of lives for Jesus.

Where did John and Charles's love for Christ and passion to see His Word preached come from?

Their momma, of course.

She may not have worn a cape or patent leather boots, but the Wesley brothers' mom, Susanna Wesley, is a hero because she literally birthed a church.

Susanna knew motherhood was tough—she delivered nineteen children in twenty-one years. Only ten of those babies survived beyond the age of two. Susanna depended on Christ with a contagious ferocity. She educated her children, launched a home church while her preaching husband was away, and took responsibility for her children's souls.

She knew better than to disciple her large brood in her own strength. When she needed time alone, Susanna sometimes pulled her apron over her head. It was her clear cue to her children to "leave mom alone." Susanna wasn't hiding under her smock for "me time," but to pray for herself and her family.[36] Those prayers bore fruit in her children's lives and multiplied to reach millions.

As mothers, we can all glean something from Susanna's approach. We can find a blueprint for how this heroine lived out her faith in some of the rules of her household:

- Subdue self-will in a child, and those working together with God to save the child's soul.
- Teach a child to pray as soon as he can speak.
- Require all to be still during Family Worship.
- To prevent lying, punish no fault which is first confessed and repented of.
- Never allow a sinful act to go unpunished.
- Teach children to fear the rod.
- Never punish a child twice for a single offense.
- Comment and reward good behavior.
- Any attempt to please, even if poorly performed, should be commended.
- Strictly observe all promises. [37]

Certainly any woman who trains her children so seriously is a hero in my book. Her sons may have made some important gains for the kingdom, but their momma led them to their secret source of strength.

We find this same pattern in the life of another Christian heavyweight, Billy Graham. Graham has preached the gospel to nearly 215 million people in more than 185 countries and territories. He has written thirty books, read by millions of readers. He has met with presidents to pray and pass on biblical truth. Gallup has frequently listed him as one of the "Ten most admired men in the world."

IN COMIC BOOKS, superheroes get strength from everything from radioactive spiders (Spiderman) to clouds of cosmic energy (The Fantastic Four), but God seems to provide strength and encouragement through the teaching and example of mothers.

Just like the Wesley boys, Graham's impact can be traced back to a quieter heroine, his mom.

Billy Graham said this about his mother, Morrow: "Of all the people I have ever known, she had the greatest influence on me. I am sure one reason that the Lord has directed and safeguarded me, as well as [my wife] and the children, through the years, was the prayers of my mother and father."[38]

In comic books, superheroes get strength from everything from radioactive spiders (Spiderman) to clouds of cosmic energy (The Fantastic Four), but God seems to provide strength and encouragement through the teaching and example of mothers.

I've heard people say that if the AIDS crisis in Africa is going to be solved, mothers will solve it. I believe that's true. Moms have what politicians, doctors, and relief organizations lack—a momma bear instinct that causes us to do whatever is necessary to protect our children's well-being.

Moms who apply that God-given tenacity might as well strap on a bright red cape, because that powerful combination allows them to become a breed of superhero that God can use to fight any evil that tries to rise against our families.

Real Moms, Real Heroes

Some of the bravest heroes I know can't leap buildings in a single bound or tap into superpowers when their human nature fails. But they press on and make a difference through their role as a mother.

When I think of heroes, I think of Sandy, whose daughter, Rene, was entrenched in a sinful lifestyle for eleven years. Through that entire season, Sandy prayed. When she was all "prayed out," she recruited her friends to pray.

As months turned into years, Sandy did not lose hope. She kept trusting God's promise to answer prayer. Rene now lives for Christ, motivating women through her position on staff at a national revival ministry. Certainly God deserves the credit for Rene's radical transformation, but He used her momma as conduit for that change.

When I think of heroes, I think of Nancy, a single woman in her fifties who never married or had children. Nancy pours love into her nieces and nephews and other kiddos in her life, shepherding them with God's truth about how they should live. She lives out the principles in Isaiah 54:1. She also encourages moms to see the kingdom value in their efforts and to press on with joy.

When I think of heroes, I think of my mom, Gini. She grew up during the rise of feminism when my grandmother was falling for the lie that career is king. But, my mom saw parenting us as her most important job, even though she worked full-time and parented alone. She never lost her joy, and she never forgot that Jesus was her source of strength.

Mom raised three kids who love the Lord, and who are now raising five grandkids to know the Lord. Two of us are involved in student ministry, and have deliberately taught young women the value of mothering—multiplying her efforts even more.

And I doubt that I would have ever written a book about motherhood if I hadn't watched my mom's example. As each of you accept God's calling to see your children as your most important ministry, her precedent gets multiplied indefinitely.

Try not to think of these heroes as a formula for the type of woman and mom you should be. At this point, you may be amped up about approaching motherhood with a new sense of purpose, and you want me to give you a checklist of exactly how to do it.

It doesn't work that way, because we are talking about Spirit-led parenting, not some oversimplified, assembly line definition of a biblical woman. I'm pushing you toward letting God into this area of your life in a bold, new way. I want you to ask God what your purpose is, and to be brave enough to find out if your answer has been fully surrendered to Him.

YOU MAY BE amped up about approaching motherhood with a new sense of purpose and want a checklist of exactly how to do it. It doesn't work that way, because we are talking about Spirit-led parenting, not some oversimplified, assembly line definition of a biblical woman.

I have no idea what plans God has for you. Maybe He wants you to homeschool your children so the responsibility of training them falls more squarely on your shoulders. Maybe He wants you to send them to public school and to intentionally equip them to be salt and light.

Maybe God is calling you to have more children. Maybe He wants you to adopt, or maybe He wants you to find ways to pour into the children who are already in your circle of influence.

I can't give you a template to adhere to. But I can urge you to take the size of your family, your methods with your children, and your own mother's heart to God's throne, and to ask Him to shape you into a brand-new creation.

Sending Out the Bat Light

Batman probably ranks high on most lists of superheroes. I certainly dig his leather pantsuit and underground lair. But my favorite thing is the bat light. When citizens were in trouble, they would shine a giant bat-shaped spotlight over Gotham, and down would swoop their hero to save the day.

I'm sending out the bat light to you, moms. Our culture is in danger of losing sight of the family's value and the critical role only mothers can play. Our children are in danger of shouldering our anger, frustration, and bitterness if we can't choose to see them as God-given blessings. And we are in danger of missing the most important ministry opportunity the Lord has ever given us.

God has sent out the bat light to parents for generations. If we look in His Word, we find countless calls to make teaching and living our faith out at home our highest priority. In verse after verse, God sends the clear signal that our children are a gift and a mission field. When we miss this message, the consequences are huge.

{ More WISE Words }

HEAR, O ISRAEL: The Lord our God, the Lord is one. You shall love the Lord your God with all your heart and with all your soul and with all your might. And these words that I command you today shall be on your heart. You shall teach

them diligently to your children, and shall talk of
them when you sit in your house, and when you
walk by the way, and when you lie down, and
when you rise. You shall bind them as a sign on
your hand, and they shall be as frontlets
between your eyes. You shall write them on the
doorposts of your house and on your gates.

—DEUTERONOMY 6:4–9

An Army of Capes

I know motherhood is tough. I know that you probably picked
up this book because you are in the middle of a discipline problem,
an identity crisis, or a string of sleepless nights. I can't do anything
to change the amount of toys in your living room, diapers in your
trash can, or time-outs you dish out on any given day. But I can help
you widen the lens through which you view your role.

When it comes to motherhood, the days go by slowly, but the
years pass at lightning speed. When we look at our kids' pictures,
we realize how fast they are growing, how soon they will leave our
nest, and how much we adore them.

The daily grind often prompts a different reaction in us. But
it doesn't have to be that way. You can see your children as a blessing all the time by meditating on God's truth. You can respond to
all mothering challenges with joy because God has promised to do

the heavy lifting. You don't have to be afraid to take your family planning to God because He is good—the things He asks of us are for our good and His glory. You can stay in the trenches of motherhood if you choose to see the kids as a mission field with kingdom stakes. You can continue to make meals, fold clothes, and go to soccer practice because you know that God uses mom math to multiply your efforts.

It probably won't be as easy as flipping a switch. You won't close this book and find that everything has been set right in your mom world. But the ball has been served directly into your court. You can make the changes to live out God's calling for mothers with greater joy, urgency, and a sense of purpose—or continue to drown in the woes that come with your role.

I hope you will choose the first option. I hope God will raise an army of mom heroes who will mother with God-given confidence, joy, and eternal perspective.

So, let's strap on our capes, moms. You can even slide into a pair of red boots. But let's rise to God's calling to swim upstream by asking God to shift our focus beyond bath time and toward ways we can use every moment in our mothering journey to point others toward Him.

Connecting the Dots

1. Who is your hero (a momma hero or otherwise) and why is that person your hero? Yes! You can list several people if you like.

2. Take a look at your own mom (or someone who was like a second mother to you). What things about her mothering would you like to emulate?

3. Susanna Wesley had her specific rules of mothering. Create your own list of rules for your kids—include spiritual and practical points.

4. Stop and think about how quickly parenting has gone so far—how much your kids have grown since you first brought them home from the hospital. If you always considered how short your years with your kids are, how would your mothering change?

5. As you wind down your study of this book, take a moment to write a prayer, committing your children and your mothering to the Lord.

A Final Word: Mom to Mom

I didn't write this book because I'm an expert on motherhood. During the months I typed it, my mom world often felt like a snow globe that someone picked up and shook with surprising violence. I've hammered out chapters while trying to ignore the smell of an overflowing diaper. I've forced myself to read and reread my own words that seeing my children as a blessing is a choice—especially when my three-year-old drew a mural on my bedroom wall with deodorant or my teething baby refused to sleep.

And even as I've studied God's clear calling to pour into my family as if they are my most important work (because they are), parts of me have longed for a "real job," an "Atta girl," or an office where they don't play Sesame Street.

I don't want you to think I have my act all together. I don't. I'm not a perfect mom, parenting perfect kids. As I seek to see my kids as a mission field and my mom responsibilities as acts of worship, I struggle, just as you do.

But as I've turned to the Bible for answers to my questions about God and motherhood, I've found the well is deeper than I ever imagined. Over and over my eyes have been opened to the radical notion that being a mom is a high and holy calling and that nothing I do will outweigh the potential impact of raising children for Christ.

As I've written this book, I've wondered where you are on your mothering journey and marveled at the number of children and families that could be affected if each of you shift your focus away from the mundane chores of motherhood and agree to participate in Nehemiah's battle plan—working with our families and working for our families to build something magnificent for God's kingdom.

So as I pen these last words, I feel I'm ending a play date. Our kids are tired and cranky, and we should wrap things up, but we want to linger and drink a little more from the refreshing well of Christian sisterhood that replenishes us for the journey.

So, let's keep talking. Here are ways you can keep the conversation going.

1. Find me online at www.beyondbathtime.com. You'll find oodles of great stuff for moms, including:

- Our Mom Blog—A cadre of moms in various stages of the journey write about mothering and what God is teaching them along the way.
- Taking the 30-day Mom Makeover—Let God teach you even more about His heart for motherhood through thirty days of devotions delivered right to your inbox.
- Connecting with a community of moms online. Give and receive hope, encouragement, and practical tools to keep mothering well.

- Links to follow me on Facebook and Twitter.
- Access to other great resources on faith and family.
- Information about my other projects for your teen and tween daughters.

2. Launch a Moms' Group

On our website you will find helps to launch a moms' ministry at your church, and ways to personalize this book as a study for your group. So log on and start reaching out to the moms around you. They need your support.

Start small with a moms' night out or play date, or start big with a mom conference focused on the principles in this book. Then hop on the blog and tell me about it. I'd love to know how God is using mom math to multiply His call to mothers.

3. Spread the Word

- **Twitter**—tweet God's truth about motherhood. Try "my children are a blessing" or "my home is my mission field" or "I'm a hero because I'm a mom" on for size. Or Tweet about this book and recommend it to other readers. Our hashtag is #Beyondbathtime and your Twitter followers may not hear about us if you don't tell them. So, Tweet away!
- **Facebook**—like us on Facebook and then commit not to use your Facebook page to vent about your children. Use it as a platform to share how God is using your ministry at home to impact others.
- **Word of Mouth**—moms are each other's greatest source of information. Don't assume that the mom next to you

in Sunday school or across the street knows God's powerful words of affirmation. Bake her cookies. Offer to take her kids for a bit and send her off to soak in a bubble bath with a copy of this book.

As I've worked on this project, I've prayed that the Lord would help me write words that matter. I hope they've made a difference in your life and will have a ripple effect in your homes, your families, and your communities. You can mother well because God has called you to do it, and He has all the strength you need to accomplish your mission.

Now, go play hide-and-go-seek, kiss chubby cheeks, start a Nerf war, and tell your kids they're a blessing. Tell them about Jesus and do it with joy. He can handle the rest.

A fan,

ERIN

Mom Makeover

Description and Day 1

You need a makeover! No I'm not referencing your mom wardrobe or the fact that you haven't had your roots done since before your oldest started kindergarten. I don't mind those things one bit. I'm talking about a makeover of your heart.

You see, being a mom can make it tough to focus our hearts on Christ. We are pulled in so many directions that spending daily quality time learning from Jesus can start to feel impossible. But I believe that if you will set aside thirty days to seek God's heart for motherhood and for your life, the changes between your "before" and "after" will be dramatic.

By signing up for this challenge, you will receive thirty days of Bible study, questions, and action steps delivered right to your inbox. I want to encourage you to keep track of what God does in your heart and in your home throughout the challenge. And be sure to hop on beyondbathtime.com to check in with other moms in the process of being made over.

Day 1: Not So Quiet Times

Be still, and know that I am God. I will be exalted among the nations, I will be exalted in the earth! —Psalm 46:10

Has the idea of a personal "quiet" time made you feel guilty during these mommy years? Cramming time for prayer and Bible study into the nooks and crannies of mothering means a) hiring a babysitter; b) locking the door and shouting something like, "Leave mommy alone! I am talking to Jesus!"; or c) waking up so early that you can only sit and stare at your Bible through tired and bleary eyes.

But the Bible doesn't say to be quiet. It says to be still.

Quietness means pulling the brakes on your life with your children. *Stillness* means taking some time to stop and acknowledge your need for God amidst the chaos, and it doesn't have to be quiet at all. In fact, adding more of God through prayer and Bible study is something you can do *with* your kids.

Action Step: Make It a Game.

Gather your flock together and practice being still. First, wiggle, jump, and dance. When you say, "Still!" have everyone freeze. Then after a few seconds of stillness offer a quick prayer that God would change your heart and your family through this challenge. Repeat. After another segment of stillness read aloud the Proverb that corresponds to the current day of the month. Have one more round of movement followed by one more "freeze." This time take turns offering a word of praise to God.

There! You've just had time with God that included prayer, praise, and Bible study. It may not have been quiet at all, but you did take the time to still your hearts before God. That's all it takes for Him to begin to change you.

A Mom's Prayer: *God, please give me more moments to spend time with You. Use this challenge to teach me Your vision for motherhood. Amen.*

NOTES

1. Rachel Jankovic, "Motherhood Is a Calling (And Where Your Children Rank)" *Desiring God*, July 14, 2011, desiringgod.org/blog/posts/motherhood-is-a-calling-and-where-your-children-rank.

2. Gretchen Livingston and D'Vera Cohn, "More Women Without Children," pewresearch.org/pubs/1642/more-women-without-children.

3. "Teenagers Want Successful Careers and Global Travel, Expect to Delay Marriage and Parenting," The Barna Group, barna.org/barna-update/article/13-culture/366-teenagers-want-successful-careers-and-global-travel-expect-to-delay-marriage-a-parenting.

4. "Motherhood Today: Tougher Challenges, Less Success," Pew Social Trends Staff, pewsocialtrends.org/2007/05/02/motherhood-today-tougher-challenges-less-success.

5. Betty Friedan, *The Feminine Mystique* (New York: W. W. Norton, 1963), 15.

6. Mary Kassian, "True Fulfillment," reviveourhearts.com/radio/revive-our-hearts/true-fulfillment/#transcript.

7. Mary Kassian, "An Undelivered Promise," reviveourhearts.com/radio/revive-our-hearts/an-undelivered-promise/#transcript.

8. "Radical Womanhood—Book Promo," youtube.com/watch?v=9e1cTly217k.

9. "Motherhood, A Sacred Task," May 12, 1985, truthforlife.org/resources/sermon/motherhood-a-sacred-task.

10. "The Sad State of Unhappy Mothers in America," Kathy Murdock, allbusiness.com/specialty-businesses/women-owned-businesses/4554305-1.html.

11. "Alcoholism: Cocktail Moms," ivanhoe.com/smartwoman/p_swstory.cfm?storyid=23387.

12. "Mom Confessions: Survey Reveals Biggest Secrets that Moms Keep," last modified August 10, 2011, huffingtonpost.com/2011/08/10/mom-confessions-survey-re_n_923394.html.

13. Nancy Leigh DeMoss and Dannah Gresh, *Lies Young Women Believe* (Chicago: Moody, 2008), 182.

14. "US Childlessness Is Up, but Racial Gaps Narrowing," the-grio.com/news/us-childlessness-is-up-but-racial-gaps-narrowing.php.

15. "Fertility of American Women: 2010-Detailed Tables," census.gov/hhes/fertility/data.cps/2010.html.

16. Luchina Fisher, "Kate Walsh, Oprah and Other Childless Stars Speak Out," *ABC News,* March 23, 2011, accessed August 20, 2011, abc-news.go.com/Entertainment/kate-walsh-oprah-childless-stars-speak/story?id=13192584.

17. Rachel Jankovic, "Motherhood is a Calling (And Where Your Children Rank)" *Desiring God*, July 14, 2011, desiringgod.org/blog/posts/motherhood-is-a-calling-and-where-your-children-rank.

18. Laura S. Scott, *Two Is Enough: A Couple's Guide To Living Childless by Choice* (Berkley, California, Seal, 2009), 2–3.

19. "The Top 100 Reasons Not to Have Kids (And Remain Childfree)," *Childfreedom: Musings on the Childfree Lifestyle in Our Child-Centric Society*, childfreedom.blogspot.com/2009/03/top-100-reasons-not-to-have-kids-and.html.

20. Rachel Jankovic, "Motherhood is a Calling (And Where Your Children Rank)" *Desiring God*, July 14, 2011, desiringgod.org/blog/posts/motherhood-is-a-calling-and-where-your-children-rank.

21. Nancy Leigh DeMoss, *Lies Women Believe: And the Truth That Sets Them Free* (Chicago: Moody, 2001), 169.

22. "World Congress of Families Congratulates Beckhams on Birth of Fourth Child—Asks for Honest Population Debate," prnewswire.com/news-releases/world-congress-of-families-congratulates-beckhams-on-birth-of-fourth-child—asks-for-honest-population-debate-126020253.html.

23. Michael Blume, "Atheists a dying breed as nature 'favours faithful,'" scilogs.eu/en/blog/biology-of-religion/2011-01-06/atheists-a-dying-breed-as-nature-favours-faithful-sunday-times-jan-02-2011-jonathan-leake-full-draft-version.

24. Kata Fustos, "The Global Muslim Population," *Population Reference Bureau,* June 2011, prb.org/Articles/2011/muslim-population-growth.aspx.

25. Michael Blume, "Atheists a dying breed as nature 'favours faithful.'"

26. Robert J. Samuelson, "The End of Europe," *Washington Post*, June 15, 2005, washingtonpost.com/wp-dyn/content/article/2005/06/14/AR2005061401340.html.

27. Lies Young Women Believe, "Raising Radicals for Jesus," Kim Wagner, liesyoungwomenbelieve.com/index.php?id=431.

28. Dorothy Kellel Patterson, "Nurturing Mothers," *Biblical Womanhood in the Home,* Nancy Leigh DeMoss, ed. (Wheaton, IL: Crossway, 2002), 168.

29. Mark Holmen, *Faith Begins at Home: The Family Makeover with Christ at the Center* (Ventura, CA: Regal, 2007), 42.

30. *World,* "Quotables," August 27, 2011, 20.

31. *Merriam-Webster,* accessed October 10, 2011, http://www.merriam-webster.com/dictionary/blessing?show=0&t=1319825108.

32. Sheri Prescott, "Viewing Motherhood as a Joy, Not a Burden," *"Hope Road,"* hoperoadblog.com/2010/04/viewing-motherhood-as-a-joy-not-a-burden/.

33. G. K. Chesterton, *What's Wrong With the World* (Glouchester, UK: DoDo Press), 67–68.

34. Holly Elliff with Bill Elliff, *Turning the Tide: Having More Children Who Follow Christ* (Niles, MI: Revive Our Hearts, 2008), 6.

35. *The Book of Common Prayer* (Church Publishing, Inc., 2010), 420–21.

36. Columba Lisa Smith, "Susanna Wesley," *Susanna's Apron,* susannasapron.blogspot.com/p/susanna-wesley.html.

37. Rev. Terri Hill, "Heroes of the Faith: Susanna Wesley," August 24, 2008,suntreeumc.org/pdf%20sermons/Heroes%20of%20the%20Faith%20Susanna%20Wesley%20August%2024%202008.pdf.

38. *Billy Graham Evangelistic Association,* billygraham.org/biographies_show.asp?p=1&d=1.

Thanks!

The core message of this book is that pouring our lives out for others is kingdom work. I know that it's true because I am the blessed beneficiary of many godly people who have invested time, resources, strength, and encouragement in me. Those people's fingerprints are all over this book and all over my life, and so to them I say many thanks . . .

My battle buddies—I am surrounded by a troop of mothers who are parenting well and with joy. Many let me pick their brains endlessly about what should be in this book. Specifically, I want to say thank you to Jill McDaniel, Bekah Menditto, Stephanie Skinner, Dree Hogue, Cindy Kimmey, Nikki Wilson, Dougetta Nuneviller, Kristie Stoddard, Keri Manes, and Dannah Gresh. You are the best moms I know.

My non-mom friends—Many of the women I know who aren't moms also graciously let me talk to them about the issues of motherhood, usually while my own two children circled around the conversation like tiny tornados. Thank you to Kendra Weatherford, Jessica Oliver, Amber Howard, Nancy Leigh DeMoss, and Paula Hendricks.

Rachel Flynn—Rachel worked endless hours as my research assistant. Like a treasure hunter, Rachel dug and dug until she uncovered just the right facts, stories, and Bible verses to make a book moms would want to read. Rachel, I am proud of the godly woman you've become.

Daniel—Daniel came into our lives as a foster son before we had children of our own. God used Daniel's presence in our home to birth a mother's heart in me. Daniel, parenting you will forever be one of the greatest joys of my life. When it comes to motherhood, you were the first one to show me the ropes.

Jason—My husband, Jason, is a great dad. Watching God teach him how to shepherd his growing flock of children is a thrill. Jason, as my colaborer in this crazy world of parenting, I want you to know how much you impress me. If your sons grow up to be just like you, the world will be a much better place. Thanks for yoking your cart to mine. It is my greatest honor to build my part of the wall beside you.

Eli, Noble, and all my children not yet born—No one shapes me into the image of Christ more than my own children. You expose my selfishness, my neediness, and my endless capacity to love every single day. If each of you grows up to love and serve Jesus, my life has been well lived. I love you forever.

ALSO BY ERIN DAVIS

978-0-8024-4586-5   978-0-8026-7394-3 ebook   978-0-8024-4585-8   978-0-8026-7393-6 ebook

Beauty is one ugly subject! It's no secret that girls struggle with feeling gross, fat, skinny, tall, short, or inadequate, thanks to distorted ideas of what beauty really is. The media is no help, with its airbrushed and enhanced images of models and movie stars. The answer isn't dieting or new clothes or surgery. The answer is found in the Word of God. Author Erin Davis, who has struggled plenty with her own body image, takes young women on a journey of discovery and love to a new image of themselves as daughters of God. She addresses issues such as how we talk to ourselves, truths about our bodies, redefining flaws, disordered eating, and true inward beauty in this honest and thought-provoking book. Journal prompts help readers dig deeper into each chapter. Young women will come to a deeper understanding of physical and spiritual beauty as they look in the mirror through God's eyes.

MOODY Publishers™

From the Word to Life

MoodyPublishers.com

FOR MOMS

978-0-8024-0448-0

978-0-8024-8152-8 ebook

Christian parents have a responsibility to make sure their children know and love God's Word. But how can you pass a love for God's Word along to your children if you struggle with it yourself? That was Carrie Ward's story. Until God gave her a plan to help her develop a consistent time in the Word, right along with her children. Readers will walk together with Carrie Ward, an everyday mama, as she journeys through the Bible with her small children—one chapter a day. As her children reenact the Bible stories readers will be able to see Scripture through the eyes of a child. Parents will learn how to impart God's truth to their children day by day, and will see its transformative power on their families. *Together: Growing Appetites for God* is an easy read and includes helpful tools for scripture memorization and charts to follow progress through the Bible.

MOODY
Publishers™

From the Word to Life

MoodyPublishers.com

978-0-8024-0644-6   978-0-8024-0642-2   978-0-8024-0643-9   978-0-8024-0643-9

Also available as ebooks

MOODY
Publishers™

From the Word to Life

www.MoodyPublishers.com

Parenting with Scripture

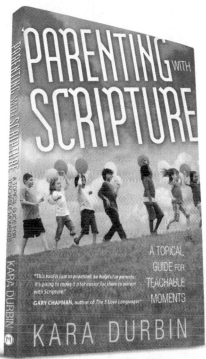

ISBN: 978-0-8024-0849-5

also available as an ebook

Parenting with Scripture aims to make you alert to opportunities to talk to your child about godly living. Furthermore, the ideas for simple discussions, Scriptures for memorization, and activities that are adaptable to your children's ages and interests will make you wonder why you didn't have this book before!

MOODY
Publishers™

From the Word to Life

www.Moody Publishers.com